# Too Cute!

# TOO CUTE!

*Cotton Knits for Toddlers*

## DEBBY WARE

*Martingale*™
& C O M P A N Y

Too Cute! Cotton Knits for Toddlers
© 2002 by Debby Ware

*Martingale*™
& COMPANY

Martingale & Company
20205 144th Avenue NE
Woodinville, WA 98072-8478
www.martingale-pub.com

## Credits

President: Nancy J. Martin
CEO: Daniel J. Martin
Publisher: Jane Hamada
Editorial Director: Mary V. Green
Managing Editor: Tina Cook
Technical Editor: Jane Townswick
Copy Editor: Karen Koll
Design Director: Stan Green
Illustrator: Robin Strobel
Cover and Text Designer: Stan Green
Photographer: Brent Kane

### Mission Statement

We are dedicated to providing quality
products and service by working together
to inspire creativity and to enrich
the lives we touch.

Printed in Hong Kong
07 06 05 04 03 02          8 7 6 5 4 3 2 1


**Library of Congress Cataloging-in-Publication Data**
Ware, Debby.
  Too cute! : cotton knits for toddlers / Debby Ware.
     p. cm.
  ISBN 1-56477-398-1
     1. Knitting—Patterns. 2. Children's clothing.
     3. Cotton yarn. I. Title.

TT825 .W373 2002
746.43'20432—dc21                    2001051417

# DEDICATION

This book is dedicated with love and affection to my friend Susan Zappone, who has such wonderful style and taste. Our friendship started with a casual conversation about knitting, and now, twenty-five years later, we still have not stopped talking—or knitting! Thank you, Susan, for teaching me how to make a French knot, for being the first to tell me about Tahki Cotton Classic yarn, and especially for your wonderful friendship.

# ACKNOWLEDGMENTS

Three people were especially helpful to me in regard to this book: Diane Friedman, who first presented the book idea to Martingale & Company; Elaine Brody, who gave me great encouragement and had lots of enthusiasm for my designs; and my editor, Jane Townswick, who taught me why authors are always thanking their editors for their hard work! I thank you all very much.

I want to thank Elinor Littleton, who has been a most ardent fan and whom I love dearly.

My mother taught me how to knit when I was young. She was a great teacher who was always patient and able to fix dropped stitches or other panicky problems I experienced during my first few projects. I wish my mother were alive to see this book. I know she would be pleased.

# CONTENTS

# INTRODUCTION

Garments for babies and small children are my favorite knitting projects. Since they are small, the challenges involved in doing extremely complicated designs do not last too long. In a short time, you can produce great-looking sweaters without becoming too frustrated or bored. And since babies can't argue with you about what you dress them in, you can let your imagination fly and enjoy creating outlandish and fun designs. When you've completed your projects, keep those leftover yarns for knitting hats and booties.

My designs for the sweaters and other garments in this book feature a generous amount of ease. I like to make boxy-shaped sweaters for babies and toddlers, since that shape is easy to knit and comfortable for them to wear. The sizes of most garments in this book are listed as 6–12 months and 18–24 months. As a guideline to choosing what size sweater to make, use a tape measure to determine the chest size of the child for whom you want to knit. Compare that measurement to the finished chest sizes listed in the project, and keep in mind that the fit of each sweater is intended to be roomy, both stylewise and for longer wear.

Whenever I design a knitted garment for babies or toddlers, I sit down with needles and yarn and start creating from there. I never use paper and pen to draw out my ideas first and then knit up a project. All I need is a vague idea in my head as to what I'm trying to accomplish. Nothing is written in stone during the creative process. I am a very carefree knitter, and I do not worry too much about having the "correct" number of stitches or the "right" gauge. Creating as I go allows me to take advantage of new ideas when they come to me, and it is the only way I know how to design.

The projects in this book are very simple, basic patterns that you can use as the basis for coming up with your own creative ideas. So loosen up, have fun, and enjoy making some bright and colorful sweaters, booties, hats, and other knitted garments for your favorite little ones. You cannot make a mistake!

*Debby Ware*

# SUPPLIES AND TOOLS

## COTTON YARN

All the projects in this book were knit with cotton yarn. My favorite yarn is Cotton Classic by Tahki. I have been knitting with it for years, and I think we are a match made in heaven. I have never found any other cotton yarn that compares to it. It knits up beautifully and is machine washable, which makes it a perfect choice for babies' and kids' knits. The wearability of this yarn is fabulous, and it comes in a wide range of glorious colors that will really get your creative juices flowing and allow you to come up with your own beautiful combinations. You don't have to stick to blue for boys and pink for girls anymore (but if you want to, Cotton Classic comes in quite a selection of each)! The labels on Cotton Classic yarns feature color numbers, rather than color names, so in each of the projects in this book you will find the numbers of the colors used in the garments shown. To make it easier to use the patterns, I have also referred to each color by a descriptive name, such as lemon yellow, bright orange, or French blue. These are my own names for the yarn colors; they are not indicated on Tahki Cotton Classic labels.

# MUST-HAVE TOOLS

Here are some of the tools on my "must have" list. They will make your knitting easier and more enjoyable.

**Bobbins.** When I'm working with several different colors of yarn on the same knitted piece, I use a bobbin for each individual yarn color. You can buy ready-made plastic bobbins in several sizes at any yarn shop. See page 20 for more information about bobbins.

**Crochet hooks.** A crochet hook makes it possible to rescue dropped stitches quickly and can be a helpful tool for weaving in yarn ends. A size G or H hook will work very well with Tahki Cotton Classic yarn.

**Gauge rulers.** Instead of using a tape measure to measure the gauge of your knitting, use an actual gauge ruler; it's easier. These small metal or plastic squares or rectangles feature a hole that is large enough for several inches of knitting to show through. The hole is ringed by both inches and centimeters, which allows you to check your own knitting gauge easily and accurately.

**Knitting needles.** You will use a few different types of knitting needles in your projects:

*Circular needles.* Circular knitting needles are available in plastic, bamboo, or aluminum and in various lengths, from 16" or 24" to 29" or 47". Circular needles are great whenever you want your knitting to form a seamless tube, such as in the Seed-Stitch Overalls on page 65. You can also use circular needles for knitting back and forth, which gives you the advantage of not having to keep track of a second needle.

*Double-pointed needles.* These are available in plastic or aluminum, and they are sold in sets of four or five, and in several lengths. I always use the shortest ones I have, because they are easier to work with when knitting small projects for children.

*Straight needles.* We have a variety of different types of straight knitting needles to choose from in today's market, from bamboo to plastic or aluminum, and they come in a variety of lengths, from 10" to 16". I like using

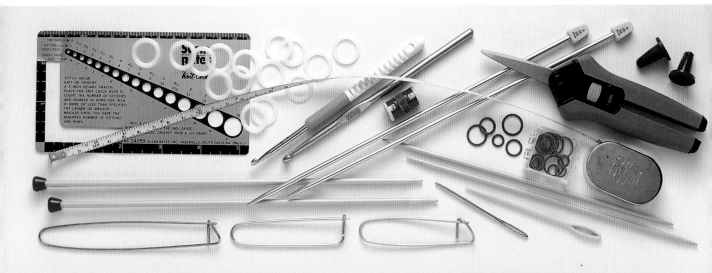

10"-long aluminum needles, since cotton yarn glides easily over them. Try experimenting with several different brands of straight needles and decide which ones you enjoy using.

**Needle gauge.** One thing I find very helpful, especially for sizing circular needles that have no size numbers on them, is a needle gauge with metric sizes on one side and imperial sizes on the other. You can insert the point of any needle into the holes and determine the size of the needle.

**Needle protectors.** To keep your stitches from "jumping off" the needle when you put your work away for any period of time, tuck the tip of each needle into a molded needle protector. Look for these at any yarn shop. Purchase several, because they tend to get lost easily.

**Row counters.** These helpful little items make it easy to keep your place while reading both charts and written instructions.

**Scissors.** I like to keep a few pairs of scissors within easy reach wherever I knit. My favorite pair fits easily into my travel bag, for easy portability. Whatever type of scissors you choose, make sure to keep the blades sharp, and never let anyone cut paper with them.

**Stitch holders.** When you need to hold stitches away from your work so you can pick them up later, plastic or steel stitch holders are great. You can find them in various lengths in yarn shops. In a pinch, you can also use a safety pin or a piece of yarn (or even an old kilt pin—remember those?). In the end, though, it's worth spending the money to purchase stitch holders that are made just for this purpose. They will make your knitting life easier.

**Stitch markers.** You can never have enough stitch markers! These are the most helpful little items, especially for making a four-point beret, where you need to count stitches to increase for the four points. You can buy stitch markers in yarn shops or from knitting catalogs. They usually come in a little box that contains sizes to fit many different sizes of knitting needles. The stitch markers I like best are little white plastic hoops.

**Tape measures.** I have been known to walk into restaurants, banks, and supermarkets with a forgotten tape measure still hanging around my neck after I have been knitting all day. When I'm working on a project, the tape measure is the first thing I pick up and drape around my neck in the morning, and I usually don't remove it until it's time to go to bed. I like the tape measures that show both inches and centimeters on the same side; they allow me to compare various measurements easily and quickly. I also have a small tape measure in a hard case that lives in my travel bag; I can take it with me wherever I go!

**Tapestry needles.** The blunt tips on tapestry needles make them perfect for sewing seams on a knitted garment. They come in both plastic and steel and in different sizes for different weights of yarn. I like steel tapestry needles and make it a habit to keep a selection of them in my knitting bag at all times.

# KNITTING BASICS

There are many different ways to cast on, knit, purl, bind off, decrease, increase, and finish. Use the following techniques for knitting the patterns in this book. For more information on knitting techniques, check your local yarn shop for good knitting reference books, or consider taking classes that will help you widen your repertoire of knitting skills.

## CASTING ON

The simplest and most common method of casting on is the one-needle cast on.

1. Make a slipknot and place it on a knitting needle. Put the tail end of the yarn around your left thumb and the other end around your left index finger. Hold both tails together with the other fingers on your left hand.

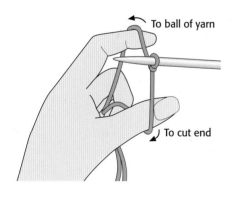

2. Insert the needle under the left side of the loop that forms around your left thumb.

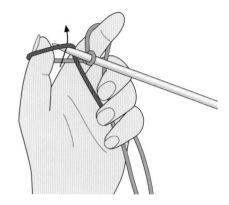

3. Gradually move the tip of the needle toward the tip of your left index finger. Pick up the yarn around your left index finger and pull it through the loop on your left thumb; then slide the loop off your thumb, completing the cast-on stitch. Pull the yarn gently to snug this stitch around the needle.

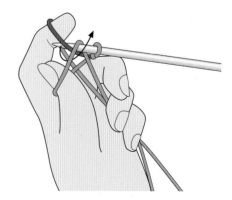

4. Repeat steps 2 and 3 to cast on the desired number of stitches.

# KNITTING

1. To do the knit stitch, hold the yarn in your right hand behind the right needle and insert the right needle from front to back into the stitch on the left needle.

2. Bring the yarn around the right needle as shown.

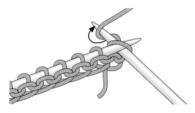

3. Bring the tip of the right needle through the stitch on the left.

4. To complete the knit stitch, slip the stitch off the left needle and onto the right one.

# PURLING

1. To do the purl stitch, hold the yarn in your right hand, in front of the right needle.

2. Insert the right needle from back to front into the stitch on the left needle, with the right needle in front.

3. Wind the yarn counterclockwise around the right needle.

4. Draw the right needle through the stitch from front to back.

5. To complete the purl stitch, slip the stitch off the left needle and onto the right one.

## INCREASING

The increases in this book are done by knitting first in the front and then in the back of the same stitch, as shown here. The process is abbreviated as K1f&b in the project instructions.

Knit into the front of the next stitch.

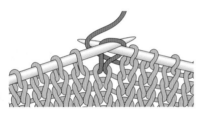

Knit into the back of the same stitch.

## DECREASING

The simplest way to decrease a stitch is to knit two stitches together. The process is abbreviated as K2tog in the project instructions.

To decrease a stitch on the wrong side of your work, purl 2 stitches together rather than knitting them.

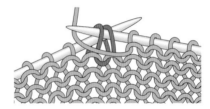

Another method of decreasing is to slip one stitch from the left-hand needle to the right-hand needle without knitting it; then knit the next stitch; then pass the slipped stitch over the just-knitted stitch. This process is abbreviated as sl 1, K1, psso.

## BINDING OFF

To bind off stitches, follow these steps.

1. Knit 2 stitches and pass the first stitch (the one on the right) over the second stitch (the one on the left). Repeat this process to bind off the desired number of stitches.

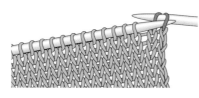

Pass first knitted stitch over the second stitch.

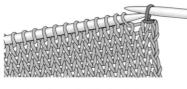

One bound-off knit stitch

2. To bind off stitches on the wrong (or purl) side of your work, repeat step 1, but purl the stitches instead of knitting them.

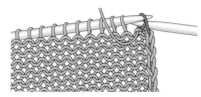

Pass first purled stitch over the second stitch.

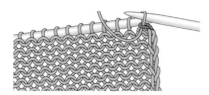

One bound-off purl stitch

## CONSIDERING GAUGE

Although the yarn amounts listed in this book are ample for each project, it is always a good idea to consider purchasing an extra skein or ball of any color that you will use a lot of. The labels on Tahki Cotton Classic yarns indicate a gauge of 5 stitches per inch; however, I like my sweaters and hats to have a tighter look, so all of my patterns specify a gauge of 6 stitches and 8 rows per inch, using size 3 US needles. To ensure that your knitted projects will be the correct finished sizes, take time to make up a gauge swatch before you actually begin knitting any project. Start by casting on 26 or 28 stitches and knit in stockinette stitch (knit one row, purl one row) until your swatch is 4" long. Lay the knitted swatch on a flat surface and use a small ruler, gauge ruler, or tape measure to count the number of stitches and rows there are in 1" of your own knitting. Take these measurements in two or three more places on the swatch to make sure that your gauge is consistent. If you count more than 6 stitches or more than 8 rows per inch on your gauge swatch, you will need to switch to a larger needle size and make another gauge swatch to make sure that you obtain the correct gauge. If you count fewer than 6 stitches or fewer than 8 rows per inch on your gauge swatch, you will need to switch to a smaller needle size and make another gauge swatch to make sure that you obtain the correct gauge.

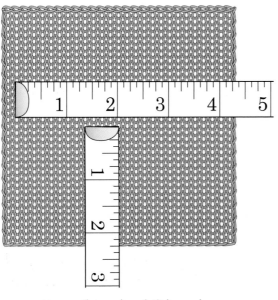

Measure the number of stitches and rows
per inch in your own knitting.

for knit rows are shown at the right side of a chart, and the numbers for purl rows are shown at the left side. When you begin knitting, follow the rows of the chart from the bottom to the top, beginning with row 1. Each different color is represented by a different color on the chart. Sometimes it can be helpful to place a ruler just under the row you are working and move the ruler up as you work through the chart.

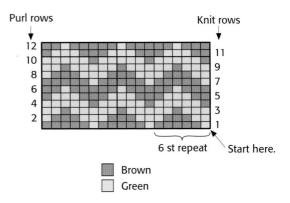

## READING CHARTS

For patterns that feature color knitting in stockinette stitch, the patterns are presented on charts, which are much easier to read than written instructions. Each square of the chart equals one stitch, and each line of squares represents one row. The knit (or right-side, abbreviated RS) rows are odd-numbered rows and are read from right to left, in the same direction as you knit. The purl (or wrong-side, abbreviated WS) rows are even-numbered rows, and are read from left to right, in the same direction as you purl. The numbers

## USING BOBBINS

When you need to knit with a few colors that are separated by wide expanses of a background color, bobbins are the perfect choice for holding the yarn in back of your work until you are ready to work with each color. Simply wind a small amount of each color of yarn around a bobbin and introduce each color wherever it is called for in the chart. When you begin working with a new color, take care to bring the bobbin color underneath the background color before you begin knitting with it; the yarns will twist together and prevent gaps between your stitches on the wrong side of your work. In the same manner, when you finish working with each color, bring the next color of yarn you want to work with underneath the bobbin yarn and begin knitting with the new color. Let the bobbin yarns hang at the back of your work when you are not working with them.

Bobbins for color-knitting

## MAKING BUTTONHOLES

I recommend the two-row method of knitting buttonholes.

1. Work the buttonhole row as indicated in project instructions, up to the point where the first buttonhole is to be placed. Bind off 2 stitches for the buttonhole. Continue working this row, spacing the bound-off stitches for each buttonhole as specified in the project instructions, and work to the end of the row as indicated.

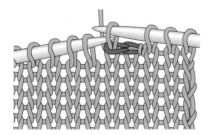

**TIP:** For the cardigans in this book, the instructions indicate to knit the buttonholes on the left front band, which is the traditional placement for a boy's garment. If you are knitting a cardigan for a girl, it is perfectly acceptable to work the buttonholes on the right front band instead.

2. On the next row, work up to the first bound off stitches. Cast on 2 stitches to complete the buttonhole using a backloop cast on: make a loop so that the yarn from the ball is in front of the yarn coming from the right-hand needle; then put the right needle into the loop and tighten. Repeat to make another stitch. Continue working this row, casting on 2 stitches to complete each buttonhole, and work to the end of the row as indicated in the project instructions.

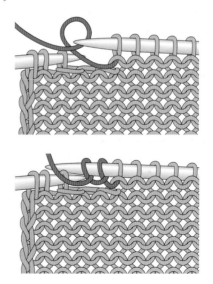

3. To make a buttonhole look more finished and easier to use, overcast the edges. Thread a tapestry needle with the same color yarn as the front band (or consider using a contrasting color for fun). Leaving a tail of yarn to weave in after you finish, * insert the needle into a stitch close to the buttonhole edge, from the wrong side of your work to the right side. Bring the needle up, insert it back down into the buttonhole, and bring it up again very close to your first stitch.* Repeat from * to * around the entire buttonhole; the yarn will wrap itself around the buttonhole opening with each overcast stitch you take. When you finish overcasting the edges of the entire buttonhole, weave the ends of the yarn through the stitching on the wrong side of your work.

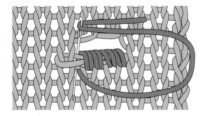

Overcast stitch the edges of buttonholes.

TIP: Buttons add a creative touch to a sweater. I almost always use vintage buttons. I have collected a great variety of beautiful ones over the years. Sometimes I spend hours choosing just the right buttons to complete a project, and occasionally I can't part with the ones that I have chosen and go on to pick still others! Vintage buttons seem to be everywhere these days, from the Internet to junk stores to yard sales, where you can usually find a glass jar filled with old buttons for very little money. After spending the time to knit a sweater by hand, consider finding some wonderful buttons for a great finish.

# FINISHING TECHNIQUES

Use the following techniques to give your knitted projects beautiful finishing touches.

## SHOULDER SEAMS

I use a very clean and neat way to sew the shoulder seams of a sweater together. It involves working from the right side of the garment, with the two bound-off edges aligned. Thread a tapestry needle with yarn that matches the knitting, and insert the needle from the back side of your work to the front, in the V of the stitch just below the bound-off edge. Then insert the needle under two strands of the knit stitch on the opposite piece and bring it back to insert it under the next two strands of the first piece. Continue in this manner along the entire shoulder seam. Keep your tension even, so that the finished seam looks just like the knitted work.

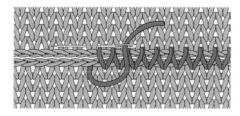

**TIP:** Consider using the ends of yarn still attached to the knitting after you finish each piece to sew the shoulder and sleeve seams. This will save you time, because there will be no need to weave those ends in later, and it will produce a neater finished look.

## BACKSTITCH SEAMS

I like to sew the side seams of a sweater and other vertical seams, such as the back seams of booties, by backstitching them. This process is similar to sewing two pieces of fabric together. Actually, if you like this technique, you can also use it to sew together an entire garment.

1. Thread a tapestry needle with yarn that matches the knitting. Secure the beginning of the seam by bringing the yarn around the seam edges twice, and bring the needle back up approximately ¼" from where the yarn last emerged, as shown.

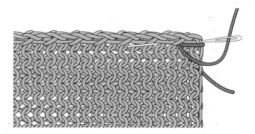

2. In one motion, insert the needle into the point where the yarn emerged from the previous stitch and bring it back up approximately ¼" to the left. Pull the yarn through. Repeat, keeping your stitches even and loose so that the finished seam will be smooth, not puckered or distorted.

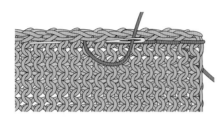

## POCKET SEAMS

To sew the edges of a pocket lining to the inside of a garment, use a tapestry needle and the same color yarn as the area you are working in. Bring the needle up through the edge stitch of the pocket lining. Then pick up the horizontal bar of the nearest stitch on the inside of the garment body and back through the next edge stitch on the pocket lining. Draw the yarn all the way through

and repeat this process around the side and bottom edges of the pocket lining, taking care to keep the tension even so no puckers appear. Weave the tail ends of yarn through several stitches on the wrong side of your work.

For projects that have patch pockets, you can sew them to the right side of the garment with a simple running stitch, which is just like a large basting stitch. Position the pocket where you want it on the front of the garment. Pin it in place with two or three straight pins. Thread a tapestry needle with a contrasting color yarn, and bring the needle up from the wrong side of the garment, leaving a tail end to weave through the stitches on the wrong side of your work later. Sew the side and bottom edges of the pocket with large, easy-to-see stitches. To finish this type of seam, bring the yarn through to the wrong side of your work and weave both of the yarn ends through several stitches.

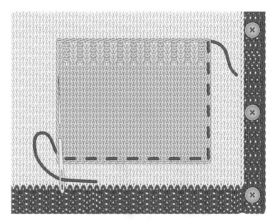

## PICKED-UP STITCHES

To pick up stitches along the edge of a cardigan front, work with the *right* side of your knitting facing you. Insert a knitting needle under each edge stitch and bring the yarn through, as if to knit. Continue picking up stitches in this manner until you have the required number of stitches on the needle.

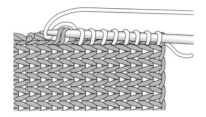

For collars, it is neater to pick up stitches with the *wrong* side of your knitting facing you so that the finished collar will cover the ridge created when you pick up the stitches. Insert a knitting needle underneath the bound-off edge stitches and bring the yarn through, as if to knit. Continue picking up stitches in this manner until you have the required number of stitches on the needle, making sure that you pick up the same number of stitches from the neck edge to the shoulder seam on one side as you do on the other.

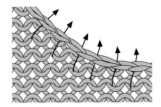

**TIP:** Sometimes picking up stitches unevenly can create a small hole or gap along the garment edge. If this happens, simply unravel your picked-up stitches until you reach the area that gaps and pick up stitches there again, inserting the needle a bit deeper into the garment edge.

## CROCHETED EDGES

You can add a single-crochet edging in a contrasting color to any of the collars in this book.

1. With RS facing, working from right to left, insert a medium-size (G or H) crochet hook into the knitted edge stitch and draw up a loop. Wrap the yarn over the hook and pull it through the first loop to secure.

   *Insert the hook into the next edge stitch, wrap the yarn over the hook, and draw the hook through the stitch.

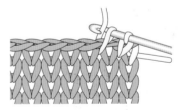

2. Wrap the yarn around the hook and draw it through both loops on the hook.

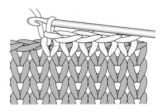

3. Repeat from * in step 1 until the entire edge of the knitting is covered in single crochet stitches.

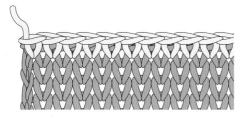

## KNITTED CORDS

Knitted cords make great additions to the tops of hats, and they are very easy to make. Simply cast on 3 or 4 stitches on a size 3 double-pointed needle. *Knit across, slide stitches back to the right end of the same needle, do not turn, and repeat from *. BO when you reach the desired length for the cord.

## DUPLICATE STITCHING

Some of the garments in this book feature duplicate stitching, which looks just like knitted stitches when finished. Using these stitches to embellish a knitted garment is easy and fun.

1. To do horizontal duplicate stitching, thread a tapestry needle with the desired color of yarn. Bring the needle through from the wrong side of your work to the front side at the base of the knit stitch you wish to cover with a duplicate stitch. Then insert the needle under the base of the knitted stitch directly above the stitch you wish to cover.

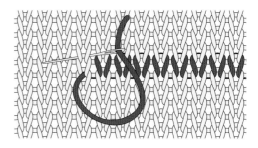

2. Bring the needle down and insert it at the base of the same knit stitch. Bring the tip of the needle out at the base of the next stitch you wish to cover, and repeat this process until you have covered all of the horizontal stitches indicated in the project. When you reach the final duplicate stitch, pull the yarn

all the way through to the wrong side and weave the end of the yarn through the back sides of your duplicate stitches.

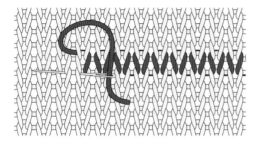

To do vertical duplicate stitching, bring a threaded tapestry needle through from the wrong side of your work to the front side, at the base of the first stitch to be covered. Insert the needle from right to left through the top of same stitch. Bring the needle down and insert it at the base of the same stitch, bringing it out again at the base of the stitch that lies directly above the one you just covered. Continue in this manner until you reach the final vertical duplicate stitch; then pull the yarn all the way through to the wrong side and weave the tail end of the yarn through the back sides of your duplicate stitches.

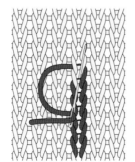

## FRENCH KNOTS

Thread a tapestry needle with the desired color of yarn, and bring the needle from the wrong to the right side of the knitted garment at the point where you wish to place a French knot. Holding the yarn down with your left thumb, wind the yarn twice around the needle (or more for larger knots). Still holding the yarn firmly, twist the needle back to the starting point and insert it close to where the yarn first emerged. Pull the yarn through to the wrong side of your knitting, creating a French knot on the surface of the garment. Take two or three whipstitches to secure the yarn on the wrong side of your work.

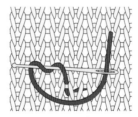

Wrap yarn around needle
2 or more times.

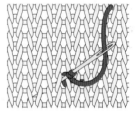

Insert yarn close to
emerging point.

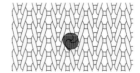

# Making Pompons

Pompons are a great way to top almost any style hat or bootie. You can make them as big or as little as you desire. Use one color of yarn, two for fun, or combine lots of colors for a confetti effect. You can buy pompon makers at craft stores. They usually come with three different-sized plastic disks that you can wrap yarn around until your pompon is as full as you want it to be. You can also cut a piece of heavy cardboard that has a height as wide as you want the diameter of your finished pompon to be. (A 3"-wide piece of cardboard will make a medium-sized pompon.) Wrap the yarn forty or fifty times around the cardboard, or even more if you want to make a very full pompon. Cut an 18" strand of yarn, slip the wound loops off the cardboard, and use the strand of yarn to tie a very tight knot around the wound loops. Use a pair of scissors to cut through the loops of yarn on either side of the tied knot, and shake the pompon hard to fluff it out. Trim the ends evenly, if necessary.

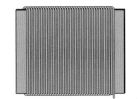

Wrap yarn 40–50 times around cardboard.

Tie a very tight knot
around the yarn.

Clip loops.
Trim evenly.

# Blocking

I like to block cardigan sweaters after I sew them together and before I add the buttons. Turn the sweater inside out and place it flat on an ironing surface. Set your iron on steam and on the cotton temperature. Place a towel over the sweater (or hat, or other garment) and, without putting the full weight of the iron down on the piece, "iron" the seams, pockets, and sleeves gently, letting the steam penetrate the towel and the cotton fibers of the knitting. I want to mention here that this is not an imperative step for the sweaters and other knitted garments in this book; they will look great without blocking. However, the square top portions of the Four-Point Berets will lie flatter if you block them in this manner.

# KNITTING ABBREVIATIONS

| | | | |
|---|---|---|---|
| approx | approximately | P | purl |
| beg | begin(ning) | pat | pattern |
| BO | bind off | psso | pass slipped stitch over |
| ch | chain | pw | purlwise |
| circ | circular | rem | remaining |
| CO | cast on | rep | repeat |
| cont | continue | rnd | round |
| dc | double crochet | RS | right side |
| dec | decrease | sc | single crochet |
| dpn | double-pointed needle(s) | sl 1 | slip 1 stitch |
| inc | increase | st(s) | stitch(es) |
| K | knit | St st | stockinette stitch |
| K1f&b | knit in the front and in the back of the same stitch | tog | together |
| K2tog | knit 2 stitches together | WS | wrong side |
| kw | knitwise | wyib | with yarn in back |
| M1 | make 1 stitch | wyif | with yarn in front |
| oz | ounce | yds | yards |
| | | yo | yarn over |

# GARMENTS

Baby Boy Argyle Cardigan

Circles Cardigan

Chicken Cardigan

Reindeer Sweater-Coat

Seed-Stitch Sweater and Overalls Set

Pastel Onesie and Button-on Booties

Swirl Skirt with Bib

Sweet Smock

# BABY BOY ARGYLE CARDIGAN

I have been asked many times to design a really boyish sweater. What could be better than the classic argyle pattern? I love this shade of blue combined with bright orange accents. My inspiration for this sweater developed from seeing those two colors together on my work table.

| | |
|---|---|
| *Size:* . . . . . . . . . 6–12 mos. (18–24 mos.) |
| *Finished chest:* . . . . . . . . . . . . 22 (26)" |
| *Finished length:* . . . . . . . . . . 12 (12)" |
| *Finished sleeve length:* . . . . . 6½ (7½)" |

## MATERIALS

- Tahki Cotton Classic (100% cotton, 50g/108yds)
  - ~ 4 (4) skeins #3882 (French blue)
  - ~ 1 skein each #3486 (bright orange), #3533 (lemon yellow), #3722 (green)
- 1 pair size 3 US straight needles
- Stitch markers
- Tapestry needle
- 4 buttons

## GAUGE: 24 sts and 32 rows = 4" in St st

*Note: The following instructions are for the smaller size. The numbers for the larger size are in parentheses. Where only 1 number is given, it applies to both sizes.*

## BACK

With bright orange, CO 70 (82) sts. Change to French blue and work in K1, P1 ribbing for 1½".

Beg St st and work until piece measures 12". BO all sts.

## RIGHT FRONT

With orange, CO 35 (41) sts. Change to French blue, and work in K1, P1 ribbing for 1½", ending with RS facing for next row.

Next row (RS): Change to lemon yellow, and beg argyle pat in St st, following chart on page 39.

*Note: Disregard the diagonal rows of stitches on the chart. You will do these in duplicate stitching after the sweater front is finished.*

Last row: After you have completed all 21 rows of chart, change to French blue and P 1 row.

Pocket opening (RS): K10, BO 15 sts, K10.

Next row (WS): P10, CO 15 sts, P10. Cont with French blue, work in St st for 18 more rows, ending with RS facing for next row.

Next row (RS): Change to green and work argyle pat on page 39 in St st as before, this time using green as background color.

*Note: As before, disregard the diagonal rows of stitches on the chart; you will complete them in duplicate stitching after the sweater front is finished.*

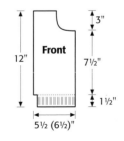

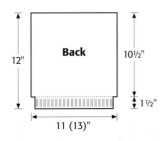

## NECK SHAPING

After you've completed all 21 rows of charted pat
on page 39, change to French blue and P 1 row.

Next row (RS): BO 5 sts, K to end.

Next row (WS): Purl.

Next row (RS): BO 5 sts, K to end.

Cont in St st to 3" above previous argyle pat. BO
all sts for shoulder.

## LEFT FRONT

Work as for "Right Front," ending with WS facing
for next row.

## NECK SHAPING

Next row (WS): BO 5 sts, P to end.

Next row (RS): Knit.

Next row (WS): BO 5 sts, P to end.

Cont in St st to 3" above previous argyle pat.
BO all sts for shoulder.

## POCKET LINING

Place sweater fronts on a flat surface, RS up, with
ribbing facing away from you. With French blue,
pick up 15 sts from 1 pocket opening. Work in St
st until pocket lining is long enough to reach the
ribbing on inside of sweater front. BO all sts. Tuck
pocket lining to inside of sweater front. Referring
to "Pocket Seams" on page 26, sew sides and bottom edges of pocket lining in place so that bottom
edge of pocket lining lies just above ribbing. Rep
to make pocket lining for second sweater front.

## POCKET RIBBING

With bright orange, pick up 15 sts across pocket
opening that is just above argyle pat. Work in K1,
P1 ribbing for 2 rows. BO all sts. Sew side edges
of pocket ribbing to sweater front. Rep to make
pocket ribbing for second sweater front.

## Sleeves

Sew shoulder seams tog, referring to "Shoulder Seams" on page 25. Lay sweater on a flat surface, RS up. Place markers 5 (5¼)" from shoulder seam on front and back. With French blue, pick up a total of 54 (56) sts for the sleeve between the markers, taking care to space them evenly. Work in St st for 5½ (6½)", ending with RS facing for next row.

Next row (RS): K2tog across row.

Work in K1, P1 ribbing for 1".

Change to orange and work 1 row in ribbing. BO all sts.

Rep to make second sleeve at other armhole edge.

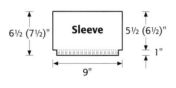

## Finishing

Sew underarm and side seams tog, referring to "Backstitch Seams" on page 25.

## Neck Band

With WS facing, use French blue to pick up 70 sts evenly all around neck edge. Work in K1, P1 ribbing for 5 rows. BO all sts.

## Left Front Band

With RS facing, use French blue to pick up 48 sts evenly along left front edge, stopping when you reach neck band. Work in K1, P1 ribbing for 2 rows.

Next row (WS): Work in K1, P1 ribbing for 5 sts, *BO 2 sts for first buttonhole, work in K1, P1 ribbing for 10 more sts*; rep from * to * twice more, BO 2 sts for last buttonhole; work in K1, P1 ribbing to end.

Next row (RS): Work in K1, P1 ribbing across, casting on 2 sts to complete each of the 4 buttonholes, referring to "Making Buttonholes" on page 21.

Work 2 more rows in K1, P1 ribbing. BO all sts. Overcast edges of buttonholes for durability.

## Right Front Band

With RS facing, use French blue to pick up 48 sts along right front edge, stopping when you reach neck band. Work in K1, P1 ribbing for 6 rows. BO all sts. Sew 4 buttons on right front band, positioning them to match buttonholes on left front band.

## Completing the Argyle Pattern

With bright orange, lemon yellow, and green, use duplicate stitches to the complete the argyle pattern, referring to the chart on page 39 and the photo on page 37 for stitch placements and to "Duplicate Stitching" on page 28.

**Argyle pattern**

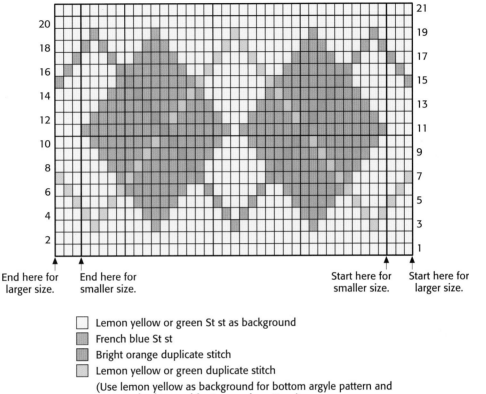

Lemon yellow or green St st as background
French blue St st
Bright orange duplicate stitch
Lemon yellow or green duplicate stitch
(Use lemon yellow as background for bottom argyle pattern and green as background for top argyle pattern.)

# CIRCLES CARDIGAN

One day I decided to use up a bunch of scrap yarns and knitted up a variety of small, decorative circles. It was so much fun, I designed this black cardigan so I could feature all of them on the same garment. Babies and small children look great in black, and this dramatic color makes a super backdrop for bright circles.

*Size:* .... 6–12 mos. (18–24 mos., 3T–4T)
*Finished chest:* ......... 22 (26, 28)"
*Finished length:* ....... 12 (12, 13½)"
*Finished sleeve length:* ... 6½ (7½, 7½)"

## MATERIALS

- Tahki Cotton Classic (100% cotton, 50g/108yds)
  - ~ 4 (4, 5) skeins #3882 (black)
  - ~ 1 skein each #3913 (purple), #3553 (yellow), #3997 (red), #3726 (green), #3062 (aqua)
- 1 pair size 3 US straight needles
- Tapestry needle
- Stitch markers
- 15 buttons

## GAUGE: 24 sts and 32 rows = 4" in St st

*Note: The following instructions are for the smallest size. The numbers for the larger sizes are in parentheses. Where only 1 number is given, it applies to all sizes.*

## PATTERN STITCH
### Seed Stitch

Row 1: *K1, P1*; rep from * to * across.
Following rows: Knit the purl sts and purl the knit sts as they face you.

## BACK

With purple, CO 70 (80, 86) sts. Work in K1, P1 ribbing for 1½ (1½, 2)", ending with RS facing for next row.

Next row (RS): Change to black and knit across.

Next row (WS): Purl.

Cont in St st until piece measures 12 (12, 13½)". BO all sts.

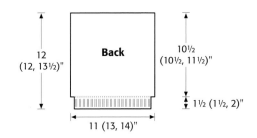

## RIGHT FRONT

With purple, CO 35 (40, 43) sts. Work in K1, P1 ribbing for 1½ (1½, 2)", ending with RS facing for next row.

Next row (RS): Change to black and knit across.

Next row (WS): Purl.

Cont in St st until piece measures 9½ (9½, 10)", ending with RS facing for next row.

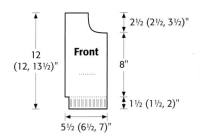

## NECK SHAPING

Next row (RS): BO 5 sts at neck edge, K to end.

Next row (WS): Purl.

Rep last 2 rows once more.

Cont in St st until piece measures 12 (12, 13½)".
BO all sts for shoulder.

## LEFT FRONT

Work as for "Right Front" up to neck shaping, ending with WS facing for next row.

## NECK SHAPING

Next row (WS): BO 5 sts at neck edge, P to end.

Next row (RS): Knit.

Rep last 2 rows once more.

Cont in St st until piece measures 12 (12, 13½)".
BO all sts for shoulder.

## SLEEVES

Sew shoulder seams tog, referring to "Shoulder Seams" on page 25. Lay sweater on a flat surface, RS up. Place st markers 5 (5¼, 5½)" from shoulder seam on front and back. With black, pick up a total of 54 (56, 60) sts for sleeve between the markers, taking care to space them evenly. Work in St st for 5½ (6½, 6½)", ending with RS facing for next row.

Next row (RS): K2tog across row.

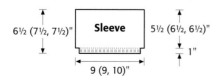

6½ (7½, 7½)"  **Sleeve**  5½ (6½, 6½)"

1"

9 (9, 10)"

Work in K1, P1 ribbing for 1". BO all sts.

Rep to make second sleeve at other armhole edge.

## COLLAR

1. With WS facing, use purple to pick up 23 sts from neck edge to shoulder seam on one side of garment. Work in seed st for 3 rows. Then BO 1 st at each end of every following row, until 3 sts remain. BO these 3 sts.

2. Rep step 1, picking up 23 sts from opposite neck edge to shoulder seam.

3. With WS facing, pick up 15 sts from 1 shoulder seam to center of back neck edge. In the same manner as for first 2 triangles, work in seed st for 3 rows; then BO 1 st at each end of every following row until 3 sts remain. BO these 3 sts.

4. Rep step 3, picking up 15 sts from opposite shoulder seam to center of back neck edge.

5. Lift up the 2 triangles on one side of neckline. With WS facing, pick up 19 sts, centering them so that 9 sts lie on either side of shoulder seam. Work in seed st for 3 rows, BO 1 st at each end of every following row until 3 sts remain. BO these 3 sts.

6. Rep step 5, lifting up 2 triangles at other side of neckline and picking up 19 sts, centering them as before, so that 9 sts lie on either side of shoulder seam.

## FINISHING

Sew underarm and side seams tog, referring to "Backstitch Seams" on page 25.

## LEFT FRONT BAND

With RS facing, use purple to pick up 50 (50, 60) stitches along the left front edge. Work in K1, P1 ribbing for 2 rows.

Next row (WS): Work in K1, P1 ribbing for 4 (4, 5) sts, *BO 2 sts for first buttonhole, work in K1, P1 ribbing for 8 (8, 10) more sts*; rep from * to * 3 more times, BO 2 sts for last buttonhole; work in K1, P1 ribbing to end.

Next row (RS): Work in K1, P1 ribbing across, casting on 2 sts to complete each of the 5 buttonholes, referring to "Making Buttonholes" on page 21.

Work 2 more rows in K1, P1 ribbing. BO all sts. Overcast edges of buttonholes for durability.

## RIGHT FRONT BAND

With RS facing, use purple to pick up 50 (50, 60) sts along right front edge. Work in K1, P1 ribbing for 6 rows. BO all sts. Sew 5 buttons on right front band, positioning them to match buttonholes on left front band.

## ADDING THE CIRCLES

Make 2 yellow, 4 red, 4 green circles, as follows:
With yellow, red, or green, CO 3 sts.

Next row (RS): K1f&b, K1, K1f&b (5 sts).

Next row (WS): Purl.

Next row (RS): K1f&b in first and last sts, and K the sts between them. Cont inc 1 st at each end of RS rows in this manner, until you have a total of 10 sts.

Next row (WS): Purl.

Next row (RS): Sl 1, K1, psso, K6, K2tog.

Next row (WS): Purl. Cont dec 1 st at each end of RS rows in this manner until 3 sts remain. BO these 3 sts.

For a complete and neat-looking circle, thread a tapestry needle with yarn tail and weave yarn through stitches on back side of circle. With purple, sew eight circles onto the sweater fronts, with large basting (or running) stitches, referring to photo on page 43 for placements. With aqua, sew a button at center of each circle.

## POCKETS

With aqua, CO 20 (20, 25) sts. Work in St st for 16 rows, work in K1, P1 ribbing for 4 (4, 6) rows. BO all sts. Rep to make a second pocket. With purple, sew a circle to each pocket with large basting (or running) stitches. Sew a button at the center of each pocket circle. With purple, sew the side and bottom edges of the pockets to the sweater fronts with large basting (or running) stitches, referring to "Pocket Seams" on page 26.

## FRENCH KNOTS

With yellow, add French knots (see page 29) to each pocket, referring to photo below for placements. With aqua, add French knots to tips of the collar triangles to attach triangles to sweater body.

# CHICKEN CARDIGAN

I love chickens, from illustrations in children's books to country fair posters to the real thing. I recently moved to a farm in Virginia, where I tend a flock of one hundred. I have been knitting different versions of this sweater for years, and this combination of deep pink and yellow is one of my favorites.

| | |
|---|---|
| *Size:* | 18–24 mos. (3T–4T) |
| *Finished chest:* | 26 (28)" |
| *Finished length:* | 12 (13)" |
| *Finished sleeve length:* | 9 (9½)" |

## MATERIALS

- Tahki Cotton Classic (100% cotton, 50g/108yds)
  - ~ 6 (7) skeins #3454 (pink)
  - ~ 1 skein each #3533 (yellow), #3711 (mint green), #3997 (red), #3214 (brown), #3223 (tan)
- 1 pair size 3 US straight needles
- Size G or H crochet hook
- Stitch markers
- Tapestry needle
- 4 buttons

## GAUGE: 24 sts and 32 rows = 4" in St st

*Note: The following instructions are for the smaller size. The numbers for the larger size are given in parentheses. Where only 1 number is given, it applies to both sizes.*

## PATTERN STITCHES
### Bobbles

With RS facing and main color, work to place for first bobble, drop main color yarn. With new color yarn, K1, P1, K1 in next st (making 3 sts from 1). Turn and K3. Turn and K3, lift second and third sts over first st. Drop the bobble yarn and pick up main color again. Work to next place for bobble, carrying the bobble yarn along the WS of work. Be sure to carry yarns loosely on wrong side to avoid distorting the knitting.

### Seed Stitch

Row 1: *K1, P1*; rep from * to * across.
Following rows: Knit the purl sts and purl the knit sts as they face you.

## BACK

With pink, CO 79 (86) sts. Work in K1, P1 ribbing for 1½ (2)".
Next row (WS): Purl.
Next row (RS): With pink, K2 (3) sts, with mint green, make bobble in next st, *K4 with pink, with mint green, make bobble in next st*; rep from * to *, ending K2 (3) sts with pink.
Cont in St st until piece measures 12 (13)". BO all sts.

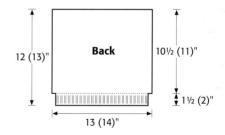

## Right Front

With pink, CO 39 (43) sts. Work as for "Back" until you have 7 rows of St st, ending with RS facing for next row.

Next row (RS): Begin working chicken pat, following chart on page 50 and referring to "Reading Charts" on page 20.

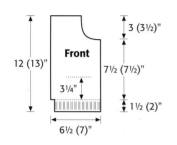

**Note:** *As you work your way through the rows of the charted design, use only the yellow or pink colors, which are the chicken and the background colors. You will add the red beak sts, the brown wing and eye sts, and the tan leg sts later with duplicate stitching and French knots. To avoid having to carry the pink background yarn across the back of your work when knitting with yellow, simply attach a second ball of pink yarn after you finish working across the yellow chicken stitches, and complete the row with the second ball of pink.*

## Pocket Opening

After you have worked row 20 of chart, make pocket opening.

Row 21 (RS): K up to yellow chicken sts and BO 25 sts for pocket opening; with pink, work to end.

Row 22 (WS): P up to bound-off pocket-opening sts and CO 25 sts with yellow; with pink, work to end.

Finish working charted pat; with pink, cont in St st until piece measures 9 (9½)" long, ending with RS facing for next row.

## Neck Shaping

Next row (RS): BO 5 sts at neck edge, K to end.

Next row (WS): Purl.

Rep last 2 rows once more.

Cont in St st until front measures 12 (13)". BO all sts.

## Left Front

Work as for "Right Front" and "Pocket Opening," following chart on page 51.

Finish working charted pat; with pink, cont in St st until the piece measures 9 (9½)" long, ending with WS facing for next row.

## Neck Shaping

Next row (WS): BO 5 sts at neck edge, P to end.

Next row (RS): Knit.

Rep the last 2 rows once more.

Cont in St st until front measures 12 (13)". BO all sts.

## Sleeves

Sew shoulder seams tog, referring to "Shoulder Seams" on page 25. Lay the sweater on a flat surface, RS up. Place st markers 5 (5½)" from shoulder seam on front and back. With pink, pick up a total of 64 (74) sts for the sleeve between the markers, taking care to space them evenly. Work in St st for 6 rows, ending with RS facing for next row.

Next row (RS): With pink, K2, with mint green, make bobble in next st, *with pink, K4, with mint green, make bobble in next st*; rep from * to *, ending K2 with pink.

Cont in St st until piece measures 8 (8½)" long.

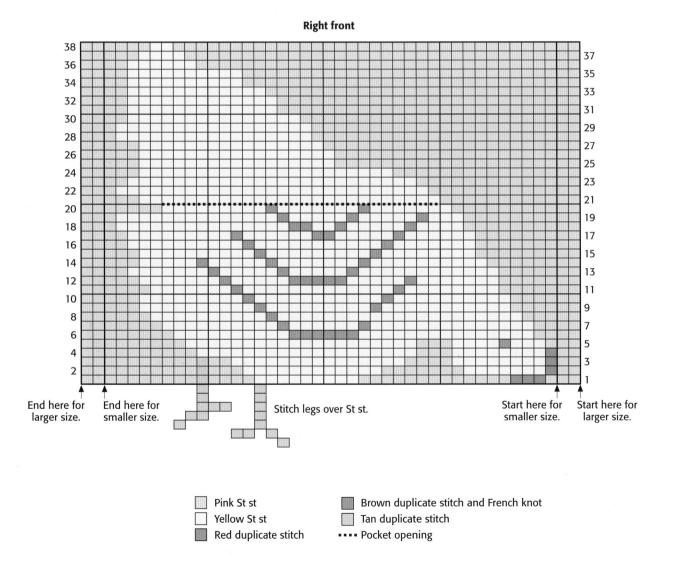

**Right front**

End here for larger size.
End here for smaller size.
Stitch legs over St st.
Start here for smaller size.
Start here for larger size.

Pink St st
Yellow St st
Red duplicate stitch
Brown duplicate stitch and French knot
Tan duplicate stitch
•••• Pocket opening

Next row: K2tog across.

Work in K1, P1 ribbing for 1". BO all sts.

Rep to make second sleeve at other armhole edge.

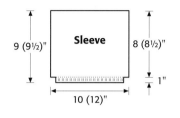

## COLLAR

With WS facing, use mint green to pick up 41 (45) sts from center of back neck to left front. Work in seed st for 5 rows. Then BO 1 st at the beg of each row, until 3 sts remain. BO last 3 sts.

**Left front**

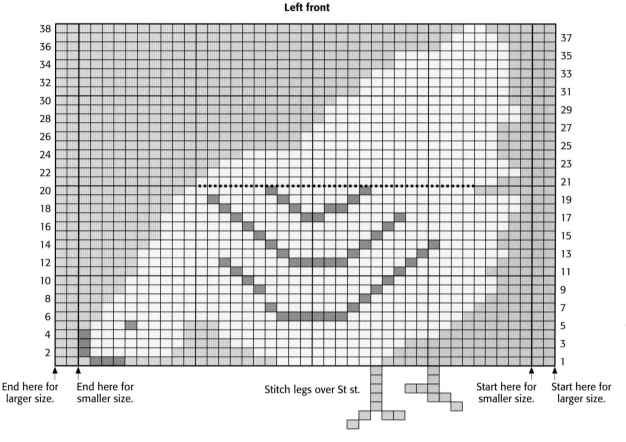

With WS facing, pick up 41 (45) sts from right front to center of back neck. Work in seed st for 5 rows, BO 1 st at beg of each row until 3 sts remain. BO last 3 sts.

With pink and a size G or H crochet hook, do a single-crochet edging around collar triangles.

## FINISHING

Sew underarm and side seams tog, referring to "Backstitch Seams" on page 25.

## POCKET LINING

With the front upside down and RS up, ribbing facing away from you, pick up 25 sts with yellow from the bound-off edge at pocket opening. Work in St st until pocket lining is long enough to meet ribbing inside sweater front. BO all sts. Rep to make pocket lining on remaining pocket opening. With yellow, sew side and bottom edges of pocket linings in place, referring to "Pocket Seams" on page 26.

## LEFT FRONT BAND

With RS facing, use pink to pick up 41 (44) sts along the left front edge. Work in K1, P1 ribbing for 2 rows.

Next row (WS): Work in K1, P1 ribbing for 3 sts, *BO 2 sts for first buttonhole; work in K1, P1 ribbing for 9 (10) sts*; rep from * to * 2 more times, BO 2 sts for last buttonhole; work in K1, P1 ribbing to end.

Next row (RS): Work in K1, P1 ribbing across, casting on 2 sts over BO sts to complete each of the 4 buttonholes, referring to "Making Buttonholes" on page 21.

Work in K1, P1 ribbing for 2 more rows. BO all sts.

Overcast edges of buttonholes for durability.

## RIGHT FRONT BAND

With RS facing, use pink to pick up 41 (44) sts along the right front edge, work in K1, P1 ribbing for 6 rows. BO all sts. Sew 4 buttons on right front band, positioning them to match buttonholes on left front band.

## DUPLICATE STITCHING

Add details to chickens, referring to "Duplicate Stitching" on page 28. Stitch the beaks with red, the wings with brown, and the legs with tan.

## FRENCH KNOTS

Add brown French knots for eyes (see page 29).

# REINDEER SWEATER-COAT

When I started designing this sweater-coat, I wanted to make a long, cozy bathrobe for small children. I love reindeer motifs that evoke the look of ski sweaters from the 1950s, so I chose my colors to go along with that look, and the bathrobe idea evolved into this diminutive sweater-coat that's perfect for chilly autumn or winter days.

| | |
|---|---|
| *Size:* ........... 18–24 mos. (3T–4T) | |
| *Finished chest:* ............ 28 (32)" | |
| *Finished length:* ........... 15 (17)" | |
| *Finished sleeve length:* ...... 7½ (8½)" | |

## MATERIALS

- Tahki Cotton Classic (100% cotton, 50g/108yds)
  - ~ 4 (5) skeins #3717 (moss green)
  - ~ 1 skein #3997 (red)
  - ~ 1 skein #3002 (black)
  - ~ 3 skeins #3525 (cream)
  - ~ 2 skeins #3358 (brown)
- 1 pair size 3 US straight needles
- 16" size 3 US circular needle
- Tapestry needle
- Stitch holders
- 6 buttons

## GAUGE: 24 sts and 32 rows = 4" in St st

*Note: The following instructions are for the smaller size. The numbers for the larger size are given in parentheses. Where only 1 number is given, it applies to both sizes.*

## BACK

With moss green, CO 84 (96) sts. Work in K1, P1 ribbing for 1½", ending with RS facing for next row.

Next row (RS): With moss green and brown, beg border pat on page 59. Refer to "Reading Charts" on page 20. Work through row 12 of charted pat.

Next row (RS): With moss green, work in St st until piece measures 7½ (9½)" long, ending with RS facing for next row.

Next row (RS): With moss green, black, and cream, beg yoke pat on page 58. After you finish the black outline stitches, cont St st in cream until piece measures 15 (17)". BO all sts.

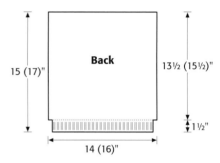

## RIGHT FRONT

With moss green, CO 42 (48) sts. Work in K1, P1 ribbing for 1½", ending with RS facing for next row.

Next row (RS): With moss green and brown, beg border pat on page 59. After you finish 12 rows of pat, work 2 rows in St st with moss green, ending with RS facing for next row.

Next row (RS): K1 (4) sts, with moss green and brown, beg reindeer pat on page 59, end K2 (5) sts. Work through row 20 of charted pat, ending with RS facing for next row.

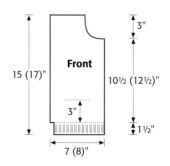

## Pocket Opening

Row 21 (RS): Cont to follow charted pat, K15 (18) sts, BO 20 sts for pocket opening, K to end.

Row 22 (WS): Cont to follow charted pat, P to bound-off sts, with moss green CO 20 sts for pocket lining, P to end.

Next row (RS): Finish working charted pat; cont in St st in moss green until piece measures 7½ (9½)" long, ending with RS facing for next row.

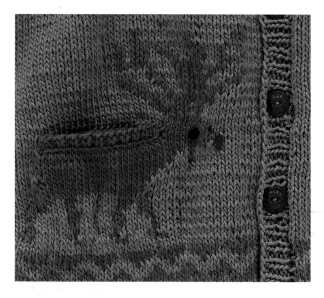

## Yoke

With moss green, black, and cream, beg right yoke pat on page 58. After you finish the black outline stitches, cont in St st in cream until piece measures 12 (14)" long, ending with RS facing for next row.

## Neck Shaping

Next row (RS): BO 5 sts at neck edge; K to end.

Next row (WS): Purl.

Rep the last 2 rows twice more. Cont in St st until piece measures 15 (17)" long. BO all sts for shoulder.

## Left Front

Work as for "Right Front," "Pocket Opening," and "Yoke," using reindeer pat on page 59 and left yoke pat on page 58, which are mirror images of patterns used for right front. End with WS facing for next row.

## Neck Shaping

Next row (WS): BO 5 sts at neck edge, P to end.

Next row (RS): Knit.

Rep last 2 rows twice more. Cont in St st until piece measures 15 (17)" long. BO all sts for shoulder.

## Pocket Lining

Place the sweater-coat fronts on a flat surface, RS up, with the ribbing facing away from you. With moss green, pick up 20 sts from 1 pocket opening. Work in St st until pocket lining is long enough to reach ribbing on inside of sweater-coat front. BO all sts. Tuck pocket lining to inside of sweater-coat front. Sew sides and bottom edges of pocket lining in place so that bottom edge of pocket lining lies just above ribbing, referring to "Pocket Seams" on page 26. Rep to make pocket lining for second front.

## POCKET RIBBING

With brown, pick up 20 sts across pocket opening. Work in K1, P1 ribbing for 2 rows. BO all sts. Sew side edges of pocket ribbing to sweater-coat front. Rep to make ribbing for second front.

## SLEEVES

Sew shoulder seams tog, referring to "Shoulder Seams" on page 25. Lay sweater-coat on a flat surface, RS up. Place st markers 4¾ (5½)" from shoulder seam on front and back. With moss green, pick up a total of 56 (66) sts for sleeve between the markers, taking care to space them evenly. Work in St st for 6½ (7½)", ending with RS facing for next row.

Next row (RS): K2tog across row.

Work in K1, P1 ribbing for 1". BO all sts.

Rep to make second sleeve at other armhole edge.

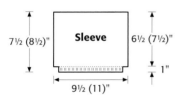

Sleeve

7½ (8½)"  6½ (7½)"  1"  9½ (11)"

## FINISHING

Sew underarm and side seams tog, referring to "Backstitch Seams" on page 25.

## NECK BAND

With RS facing, use brown yarn and circular needles to pick up 80 (90) sts around neck edge.

Work K1, P1 ribbing, increasing to 93 sts on first row. Work back and forth (not in the round) in K1, P1 ribbing for 6 rows. BO all sts.

## LEFT FRONT BAND

With RS facing, use moss green to pick up 68 (78) sts evenly along left front edge, stopping when you reach neck band. Work in K1, P1 ribbing for 2 rows.

Next row (WS): Work in K1, P1 ribbing for 3 sts, *BO 2 sts for first buttonhole, work in K1, P1 ribbing for 10 (12) more sts*; rep from * to * 4 times more, BO 2 sts for last buttonhole, work in K1, P1 ribbing to end.

Next row (RS): Work in K1, P1 ribbing across, casting on 2 sts to complete each of the 6 buttonholes, referring to "Making Buttonholes" on page 21.

Work 2 more rows in K1, P1 ribbing. BO all sts. Overcast edges of buttonholes for durability.

## RIGHT FRONT BAND

With RS facing, use moss green to pick up 68 (78) sts along the right front edge, stopping when you reach neck band. Work in K1, P1 ribbing for 6 rows. BO all sts. Sew 6 buttons on right front band, positioning them to match buttonholes on left front band.

## FRENCH KNOTS

With red, add a French-knot nose to each reindeer. With black, add French-knot eyes to each reindeer. See "French Knots" on page 29.

**Back yoke**

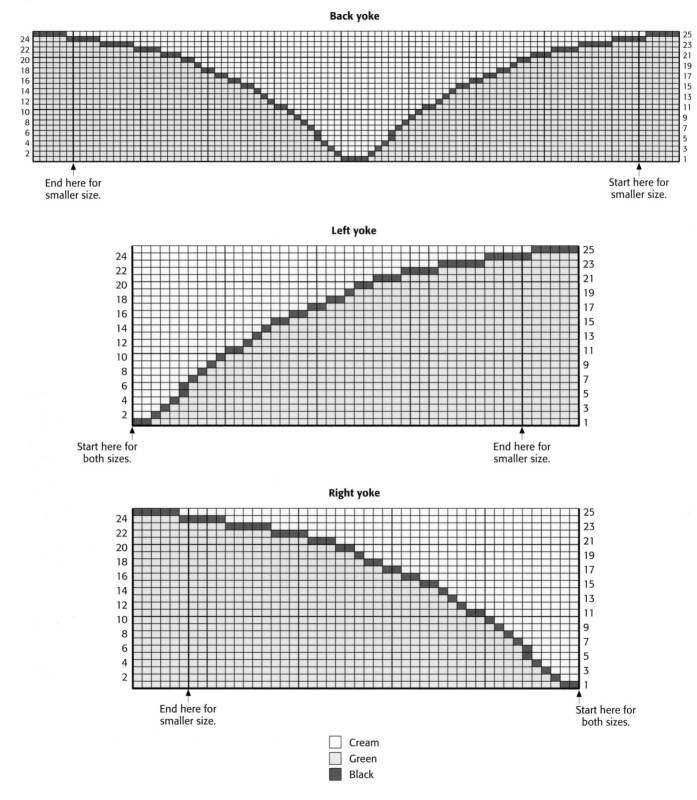

End here for
smaller size.

Start here for
smaller size.

**Left yoke**

Start here for
both sizes.

End here for
smaller size.

**Right yoke**

End here for
smaller size.

Start here for
both sizes.

Cream
Green
Black

**Right front**

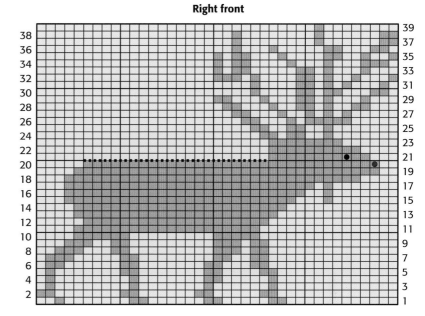

**Border pattern**

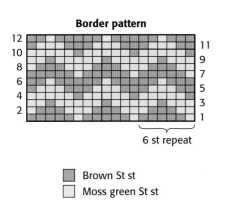

6 st repeat

Brown St st
Moss green St st

**Left front**

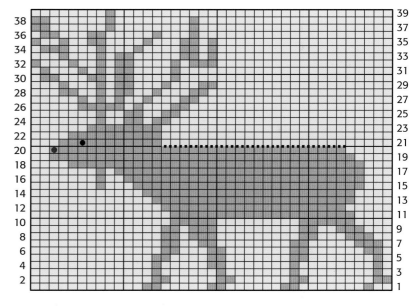

Brown St st      ▪▪▪▪ Pocket opening
Moss green St st   ● Red French knot
                    ● Black French knot

# Seed-Stitch Sweater and Overalls Set

I love baggy pants on babies, and the seed stitch has always been my favorite. I think this combination of colors and textures is very cute for boys or girls.

# SEED-STITCH SWEATER

**Size:** . . . . . . . . . 6–12 mos. (18–24 mos.)
**Finished chest:** . . . . . . . . . . . . 26 (30)"
**Finished length:** . . . . . . . . . . 12 (13)"
**Finished sleeve length:** . . . . . . . . 7 (8)"

## MATERIALS

- Tahki Cotton Classic (100% cotton, 50g/108yds)
  - ~ 5 (5) skeins #3553 (yellow)
  - ~ 1 skein each #3401 (orange), #3723 (green), #3454 (pink)
- 1 pair size 3 US straight needles
- 16" size 3 US circular needle
- Stitch holder
- Tapestry needle
- Stitch markers
- 3 buttons

# GAUGE: 24 sts and 32 rows = 4" in St st

*Note: The following instructions are for the smaller size. The numbers for the larger size are given in parentheses. Where only 1 number is given, it applies to both sizes.*

# PATTERN STITCHES
## Seed Stitch
Row 1: *K1, P1*; rep from * to * across.

Following rows: Knit the purl sts and purl the knit sts as they face you.

## Garter Stitch
Knit all rows.

# BACK
With green, CO 80 (90) sts. Work in K1, P1 ribbing for 1¼", ending with RS facing for next row.

Next row (RS): With orange, K across. Rep this row 3 times for 4 rows of garter st.

Next row (RS): With yellow, K across.

Next row (WS): Purl.

Cont in St st for 7 rows.

Next row (WS): Work in seed st across. Cont in seed st until piece measures 3¼" above ribbing, ending with RS facing for next row.

Next row (RS): With orange, work 4 rows in seed st.

Next row (RS): With yellow, work in seed st until entire piece measures 12 (13)" long. BO all sts.

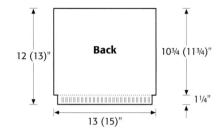

# FRONT
With green, CO 80 (90) sts. Work in K1, P1 ribbing for 1¼", ending with RS facing for next row.

Next row (RS): With orange, K across. Rep this row 3 times for 4 rows of garter st.

Next row (RS): With yellow, K across.

Next row (WS): Purl.

Cont in St st for 7 rows.

Next row (WS): Work in seed st across.

Cont in seed st until piece measures 3¼" above ribbing, ending with RS facing for next row.

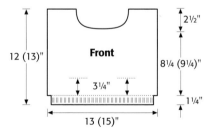

## POCKET OPENING

Next row (RS): With orange, work 12 (14) sts in seed st, BO 14 (16) sts for first pocket opening, work 28 (30) sts in seed st, BO 14 (16) sts for second pocket opening, work 12 (14) sts in seed st.

Next row (WS): Work 12 (14) sts in seed st, CO 14 (16) sts, work 28 (30) sts in seed st, CO 14 (16) sts, work 12 (14) sts in seed st.

Cont in seed st until piece measures 9½ (10½)" long, ending with RS row facing for next row.

## LEFT NECK SHAPING

Next row (RS): Work 40 (45) sts in seed st, place rem 40 (45) sts on st holder.

Next row (WS): BO 5 sts at neck edge, work in seed st to end.

Next row (RS): Work 35 (40) sts in seed st.

Next row (WS): BO 5 sts at neck edge, work in seed st to end.

Cont in seed st until entire piece measures 12 (13)" long. BO all sts for shoulder.

## RIGHT NECK SHAPING

Pick up 40 (45) sts from st holder.

Next row (RS): BO 5 sts at neck edge, work in seed st to end.

Next row (WS): Work in seed st across.

Next row (RS): BO 5 sts at neck edge, work in seed st to end.

Next row (RS): Cont in seed st until entire piece measures 12 (13)" long. BO all sts for shoulder.

## SLEEVES

Referring to "Shoulder Seams" on page 25, sew shoulder seams tog, leaving 2½" of left shoulder seam unsewn for neck opening. Place st markers 4 (4½)" from shoulder seam on front and back. With yellow, pick up a total of 48 (54) sts for sleeve between the markers, taking care to space them evenly. Work in seed st until sleeve measures 5½ (6½)" long, ending with RS facing for next row.

Next row (RS): With orange, work 4 rows in garter st.

Next row (RS): With green, K2tog across.

Cont in K1, P1 ribbing for 1". BO all sts. Rep to make second sleeve at other armhole edge.

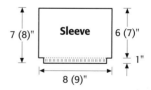

## FINISHING

Sew underarm and side seams tog, referring to "Backstitch Seams" on page 25.

## POCKET LINING

With RS facing and ribbing facing away, use yellow to pick up 14 (16) sts from pocket opening. Work in St st until pocket lining is long enough to reach the bottom of seed st area on sweater front. BO all sts. Sew pocket lining in place, referring to "Pocket Seams" on page 26. Rep to make second pocket lining at remaining pocket opening.

## BUTTONHOLE BAND

With RS facing, use green to pick up 12 sts along left front shoulder opening and work 1 row in K1, P1 ribbing.

Next row (RS): Cont in K1, P1 ribbing as established, work first st, *BO 2 sts for first buttonhole, work 2 more sts*; rep from * to * once, BO 2 sts for third buttonhole, work last st in K1, P1 ribbing, as established.

Next row (WS): Work in K1, P1 ribbing across, casting on 2 sts to complete each of the 3 buttonholes, referring to "Making Buttonholes" on page 21.

Overcast edges of buttonholes for durability.

## NECK RIBBING

With RS facing, use green and circ needle to pick up 80 (84) sts starting at top of buttonhole band, along front and back neck edge and remaining edge at left back shoulder opening. Working back and forth (not in the round), work 3 rows in K1, P1 ribbing. BO all sts.

Sew 3 buttons to the ribbing at back of left shoulder opening, matching them to buttonholes on front buttonhole band.

## DUPLICATE STITCHING AND FRENCH KNOTS

With pink, do duplicate stitching to decorate the St st area with zigzag pat, following chart below.

*Note: For the smaller size, the 12-st pattern repeat is repeated 6 times across the front and 6 times across the back. For the larger size, the 12-st pattern repeat is repeated 7 times across the front and 7 times across the back. Following the chart, add green French knots.*

**Zigzag pattern**

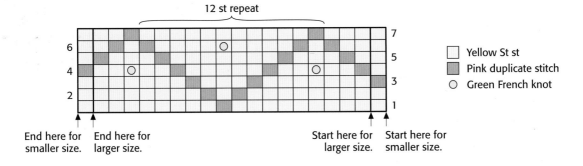

# SEED-STITCH OVERALLS

**Size:** . . . . . . . . . 6–12 mos. (18–24 mos.)
**Finished hip:** . . . . . . . . . . . . . . 32 (36)"
**Finished length:** . . . . . . . . 12½ (12½)"

## MATERIALS

- Tahki Cotton Classic (100% cotton, 50g/108yds)
  - ~ 5 (6) skeins of #3553 (yellow)
  - ~ 1 skein each #3723 (green), #3401 (orange), #3454 (pink)
- 1 pair size 3 US straight needles
- 24" size 3 US circular needle
- Stitch holder
- Stitch marker
- Tapestry needle
- 3 buttons

## GAUGE: 24 sts and 32 rows = 4" in St st

*Note: The following instructions are for the smaller size. The numbers for the larger size are given in parentheses. Where only 1 number is given, it applies to both sizes.*

## PATTERN STITCHES

### Seed Stitch

Row 1: *K1, P1*; rep from * to * across.
Following rows: Knit the purl sts and purl the knit sts as they face you.

### Garter Stitch

Knit all rows.

(See pages 88–93 for beret instructions)

## Legs

With green, CO 48 (54) sts. Work in K1, P1 ribbing for 1½", ending with RS facing for next row.

Next row (RS): With orange, work 4 rows in garter st.

Next row (RS): With yellow, inc 1 st in each st across—96 (108) sts. Refer to "Increasing" on page 18. Cont in seed st until piece measures 3¾" above cuff, ending with RS facing for next row.

## Crotch

BO 3 sts at beg of next 2 rows. Dec 1 st each side every other row 3 times to 84 (96) sts. Slip leg sts onto a st holder or spare needle.

Rep to make second leg.

## Joining the Legs

Finish second leg to same row as first leg and slip sts onto circ needle. Without cutting yarn, cont working in seed st across sts for first leg, joining them into a circle containing 168 (192) sts.

*Note: Place a stitch marker to indicate where you join 2 legs tog. This will become the center back of the overalls.*

Cont in seed st until piece measures 10".

Next row: Attach a new ball of yellow and beg working back and forth in seed st, rather than in the round, for 1" to create the opening at center back of overalls.

Next row: K2 tog across, decreasing to 84 (96) sts.

Next row: Knit.

Next row: K2 sts, BO 2 sts for buttonhole, K to end.

Next row: K up to bound-off sts for buttonhole, CO 2 sts, K to end. Work in garter st for 2 more rows. BO all sts.

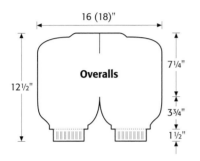

## STRAPS

With green, CO 14 (16) sts. Work in K1, P1 ribbing for 6 rows.

Next row: Work in K1, P1 ribbing for 6 (7) sts, BO 2 sts for buttonhole, work in K1, P1 ribbing to end.

Next row: Work in K1, P1 ribbing for 6 (7) sts, CO 2 sts, work in K1, P1 ribbing to end.

Cont in K1, P1 ribbing for 16 (17)" or desired length of strap. BO all sts. Rep to make second strap.

## FINISHING

Sew a button at center back of overalls. Sew 2 more buttons on front, positioning them in garter st area and at midpoint of each leg (see photo on page 65).

Sew straps to back of the overalls, positioning ends at bottom of garter st area and at midpoint of each leg.

# PASTEL ONESIE AND BUTTON-ON BOOTIES

I wanted to include an infant outfit in this collection, and onesies are fun to knit up. These soft blues and pinks are perfect for both baby boys and baby girls.

# PASTEL ONESIE

| | |
|---|---|
| *Size:* | Newborn–3 mos. (6–12 mos.) |
| *Finished chest:* | 20 (22)" |
| *Finished sleeve length:* | 6½ (7½)" |
| *Overall finished length:* | 23 (26)" |
| *Finished leg length:* | 9 (10)" |

## MATERIALS

- Tahki Cotton Classic (100% cotton, 50g/108yds)
  - ~ 6 (7) skeins #3841 (baby blue)
  - ~ 1 skein each #3443 (pale pink), #3772 (mint green), #3454 (bright pink), #3001 (white)
- 1 pair size 3 US straight needles
- Stitch holder
- Stitch markers
- Tapestry needle
- 12 buttons

## GAUGE: 24 sts and 32 rows = 4" in St st

*Note: The following instructions are for the smaller size. The numbers for the larger size are in parentheses. Where only 1 number is given, it applies to both sizes.*

## PATTERN STITCH
### Seed Stitch

Row 1: *K1, P1*; rep from * to * across.

Following rows: Knit the purl sts and purl the knit sts as they face you.

## GARMENT BACK
### Left Leg

With mint green, CO 23 (24) sts. Work in K1, P1 ribbing for 1", ending with WS facing for next row.

Next row (WS): With baby blue, knit.

Next row (RS): With mint green, *K1, sl 1 wyib*; rep from * to * across.

Next row (WS): With mint green, *P1, sl 1 wyib*; rep from * to * across.

Next row (RS): With baby blue, knit.

Next row (WS): Purl.

Next row (RS): K2 (0) sts, inc 1 st in each st across to last st, K1 (0)—43 (48) sts.

Work in St st until left leg measures 8 (9)" long, ending with RS facing for next row. Put these sts on a st holder.

### Right Leg

Work as for "Left Leg," ending with RS facing for next row.

### Crotch

Next row (RS): K across 43 (48) sts of right leg, CO 2 sts for crotch, without cutting the yarn, K 43 (48) sts of left leg from st holder—88 (98) sts. Cont in St st until crotch depth measures 8 (9)", ending with RS facing for next row.

Next row (RS): For smaller size only: With baby blue, K4, *K1, (K2tog) twice*; rep from * to * across, ending K4—56 sts. For larger size only: K1, *K1, K2tog*; rep from * to * across, ending K1—66 sts.

## Waistband

With mint green, work in K1, P1 ribbing for 1", ending with RS facing for next row.

## Yoke

Next row (RS): With pale pink, work in St st for 5 (6)", ending with RS facing for next row.
Next row (RS): BO all sts.

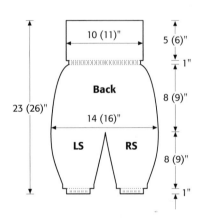

## GARMENT FRONT

Work as for "Garment Back," until crotch depth measures 1 (1½)", ending with RS facing for next row. Next you will divide for front opening.

## Left Front

Next row (RS): With baby blue, K44 (49) sts and put remaining 44 (49) sts on a st holder.

Turn and cont in St st, without shaping, until crotch depth measures 8 (9)", ending with RS facing for next row.

Next row (RS): For smaller size only: K2tog, *K1, (K2tog) twice*; rep from * to * across, ending K2tog—26 sts. For larger size only: K2, *K1, (K2tog) twice*; rep from * to * across, ending K2—31 sts.

### Waistband

With mint green, work in K1, P1 ribbing for 1", ending with RS facing for next row.

### Yoke

Next row (RS): With pale pink, work in St st until yoke measures 2½ (3½)" above waistband ribbing, ending with WS facing for next row.

### Neck Shaping

Next row (WS): BO 5 sts, P to end.
Cont in St st, dec 1 st at neck edge on next 5 (6) rows—16 (20) sts remaining.
Cont in St st until yoke measures 5 (6)" long above waistband ribbing, ending with RS facing for next row. BO all sts for shoulder.

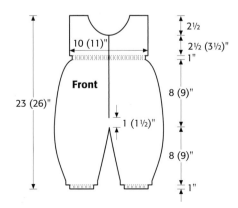

## Right Front

Work as for "Left Front" until yoke measures 2½ (3½)" above waistband ribbing, ending with RS facing for next row.

### Neck Shaping

Next row (RS): BO 5 sts, K to end.

Cont in St st, dec 1 st at neck edge on next 5 (6) rows—16 (20) sts remaining.

Cont in St st until yoke measures 5 (6)" above waistband ribbing, ending with RS facing for next row. BO all sts for shoulder.

## Sleeves

Sew shoulder seams tog, referring to "Shoulder Seams" on page 25. Lay garment on a flat surface with RS facing. Place st markers 4 (4½)" from shoulder seam on front and back. With baby blue, pick up a total of 48 (54) sts for sleeve between the markers, taking care to space them evenly. Work in St st for 5 (6)", ending with WS facing for next row.

Next row (WS): Knit.

Next row (RS): With mint green, *K1, sl 1 wyib*; rep from * to * across.

Next row (WS): With mint green, *P1, sl 1 wyib*; rep from * to * across.

Next row (RS): With baby blue, knit.

Next row (WS): With mint green, *P1, sl 1 wyib*; rep from * to * across.

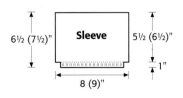

6½ (7½)"  **Sleeve**  5½ (6½)"

1"

8 (9)"

Next row (RS): K2tog across, work in K1, P1 ribbing for 1", BO all sts.

Rep to make second sleeve at other armhole edge.

## Left Front Band

With RS facing and using mint green, pick up 66 (73) sts along the left front edge. Work in seed st for 3 rows.

Next row (RS): Work 2 (3) sts in seed st as established, *BO 2 sts for first buttonhole, work 10 (11) sts in seed st*; rep from * to * 4 more times, BO 2 sts for last buttonhole, work 2 (3) sts in seed st.

Next row (WS): Work in seed st across, casting on 2 sts to complete each of the 6 buttonholes, referring to "Making Buttonholes" on page 21.

Cont in seed st for 2 more rows, BO all sts.

Overcast edges of buttonholes for durability.

## Right Front Band

With RS facing and using mint green, pick up 66 (73) sts along the right front edge. Work in seed st for 7 rows. BO all sts. Sew 6 buttons on right front band, positioning them to match buttonholes on left front band.

## Finishing

Sew side seams, inside leg seams, and underarm seams tog, referring to "Backstitch Seams" on page 25.

Sew a button at each side seam of each leg ribbing. Also sew a button at center point of front leg ribbings.

## NECK EDGING

With mint green and a size G or H crochet hook, single crochet around neckline, starting and ending at front bands and referring to "Crocheted Edges" on page 27.

## DUPLICATE STITCHING

Decorate yoke, crotch, and knee areas with duplicate stitching, following chart below and referring to "Duplicate Stitching" on page 28. Make sure to position motifs directly across from each other as you stitch them on opposite garment fronts. Use baby blue and pale pink for yoke, bright pink and mint green for crotch area, and pale pink and white for knee areas.

**Duplicate stitch pattern**

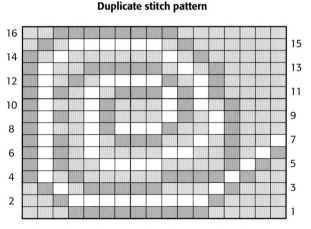

Refer to photo on page 71 for alternate color placement.

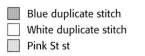

Blue duplicate stitch
White duplicate stitch
Pink St st

# BUTTON-ON BOOTIES

*Size:* . . . . . . . . . . . . Newborn–12 mos.

## MATERIALS

- Tahki Cotton Classic (100% cotton, 50g/108yds)
  - ~ Leftover colors from the onesie: #3841 (baby blue), #3443 (pale pink), #3772 (mint green), and #3454 (bright pink)
- 1 pair size 3 US straight needles
- Stitch holders
- Tapestry needle

**GAUGE:** 24 sts and 32 rows = 4" in St st

*Note: These booties are generous in size and can be used with either size onesie, if desired.*

## PATTERN STITCH
### Garter Stitch
K all rows.

## TOP
With pink, CO 46 sts. Work garter st for 2 rows.

Next row: K8, BO 2 sts for buttonhole, K12, BO 2 sts for buttonhole, K12, BO 2 sts for buttonhole, K8.

Next row: K8, CO 2 sts to complete buttonhole, K12, CO 2 sts for buttonhole, K12, CO 2 sts for buttonhole, K8.

Cont in garter st for 8 more rows. Cut the yarn.

## INSTEP
Place first 18 sts on a st holder. Join a new strand of pale pink yarn, K across next 10 sts for instep, place next 18 sts on a st holder, turn work.

Next row: K across the 10 instep sts.

Cont working the 10 instep sts in garter st for 11 rows. Cut the yarn.

Place first 18 sts on st holder onto needle. Join with baby blue, K across 18 sts, pick up 12 sts along side edge of pale pink instep, K4, K2tog, K4 across 10 instep sts, pick up 12 sts along other side edge of pale pink instep, K18 sts from second st holder—69 sts.

Work in garter st for 16 rows, ending with WS facing for next row.

## WELT
With WS facing, *sl first st from left to right needle; count down 3 ridges on WS of the baby blue garter st rows; pick up and K the top loop of the first st on this ridge; pass the first st over the new st*; rep from * to *—69 sts.

Next row: Knit.

## SOLE
Row 1: With mint green, K1, (K2tog, K29, K2tog, K1) twice—65 sts.

Row 2: K30, K2tog, K1, K2tog, K30—63 sts.

Row 3: K1, (K2tog, K27, K2tog) twice—59 sts.

Row 4: K27, K2tog, K1, K2tog, K27—57 sts.

Row 5: K26, K2tog, K1, K2tog, K26—55 sts. BO all sts.

Rep from "Top" to make second bootie.

## FINISHING
Sew seams of booties tog, referring to "Backstitch Seams" on page 25.

Overcast edges of buttonholes for durability, referring to "Making Buttonholes" on page 21.

With bright pink and mint green, make two pompons. Refer to "Making Pompons" on page 30.

Button the booties onto the onesie.

# Swirl Skirt with Bib

My friend Allison Dorriss suggested that I make a little skirt and sweater set. Well, I got as far as the skirt! Then I topped it with this darling bib.

| | |
|---|---|
| *Size:* | . . . . . . . . . . . . 18–24 mos. (3T–4T) |
| *Finished waist:* | . . . . . . . . . . . . 20 (22)" |
| *Finished skirt width:* | . . . . . . . 46 (46)" |
| *Finished skirt length:* | . . . . . . . . 7 (8)" |

## MATERIALS

- Tahki Cotton Classic (100% cotton, 50g/108yds)
  - ~ 5 (6) skeins #3997 (red)
  - ~ 1 skein each #3450 (pink), #3726 (green), #3553 (yellow), #3062 (teal)
- 24" size 3 US circular needle
- 1 pair size 3 US straight needles
- Stitch holder
- Tapestry needle
- Stitch marker
- 2 buttons
- 1 size G or H crochet hook

## GAUGE: 24 sts and 32 rows = 4" in St st

*Note: The following instructions are for the smaller size. The numbers for the larger size are in parentheses. Where only 1 number is given, it applies to both sizes.*

## SKIRT

With circ needle and red, CO 280 sts. Place st marker on right needle and join CO sts tog, making sure sts do not become twisted on needle. Work in St st (K each rnd on a circ needle) for 1¼".

Next rnd: P to form hemline.

Next rnd: Cont in St st (K each rnd) until piece measures 1½" above hemline.

Next rnd: With pink, knit.

Next rnd: Purl.

Next rnd: Knit. Cont in St st for 8 more rounds.

Next rnd: Purl.

With red, cont in St st until piece measures 5" long, taking care to end at beg of rnd.

## SPLITTING FOR CENTER BACK

Turn and work back and forth in St st until piece measures 7 (8)" or desired length to waist, ending with RS facing for next row.

Next row (RS): K2tog, K2tog, BO,*K2tog, BO*; rep from * to * until all sts are bound off.

## WAISTBAND

With red and a size G or H crochet hook, work 80 (88) sc sts around the top edge of the skirt. Rep for 5 more rows. Cut the yarn and thread it through a tapestry needle; weave yarn end through stitches on inside of waistband.

Starting at top of waistband on RS of center back, crochet a chain loop of 8 sts; attach loop at bottom of waistband.

**TIP:** You can adjust the fit of the waistband by crocheting loosely or tightly, as desired.

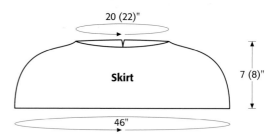

## BIB

With straight needles and red, CO 36 sts.

Rows 1, 3, 7, 11, 15, 19, 23, 25, 27 (RS): Knit.

Row 2 and WS rows up to row 28: K3, P6, K3, P center sts, K3, P6, K3.

Rows 5, 9, 13, 17, 21 (RS): K12, K1f&b (1 inc), K center sts, K1f&b (1 inc), K12.

Keeping the 12 sts on each side in pat as established, work 22 center sts in garter st for 4 rows, ending with WS facing for next row.

Next row (WS): Work first 12 sts in pat and put these sts on a st holder; BO 22 center sts, work last 12 sts in pat.

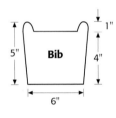

## RIGHT FRONT TAB

Next row (RS): Work 5 sts in pat as established, BO 2 sts for buttonhole, work 5 sts in pat.

Next row (WS): Work in pat as established, casting on 2 sts to complete buttonhole, referring to "Making Buttonholes" on page 21.

Next row (RS): BO 2 sts, work to end.

BO 2 sts at beg of next 3 rows. BO all sts.

Overcast edges of buttonholes for durability.

## LEFT FRONT TAB

Pick up 12 sts from st holder and work as for "Right Front Tab."

## BACK STRAPS

With straight needles and red, CO 12 sts.

Row 1 (WS): K3, P6, K3.

Row 2 (RS): K across.

Cont in pat as established until strap measures 10½". BO all sts. Rep to make second strap.

## FINISHING

Turn under the hem at the lower edge of the skirt and stitch it in place, referring to "Pocket Seams" on page 25.

Sew lower edge of bib to waistband, matching center fronts. Sew straps to waistband, approximately 1" from center back.

Sew a button to end of each strap. Sew a button to waistband at left edge of center back opening.

## DUPLICATE STITCHING AND FRENCH KNOTS

Referring to charts on page 79, decorate straps and pink border area on skirt with green, yellow, and teal duplicate stitching. Add teal and yellow French knots as indicated on chart (page 29).

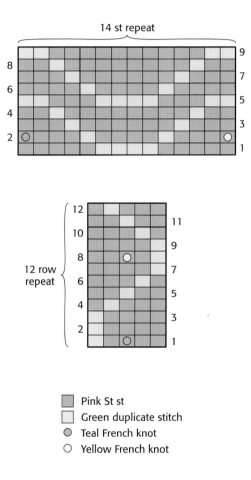

Pink St st
Green duplicate stitch
Teal French knot
Yellow French knot

# Sweet Smock

My love of smocking and knitted lace (not crocheted!) inspired me to create this sweet little sweater.

*Size:* . . . . . . . . . 6–12 mos. (18–24 mos.)
*Finished chest:* . . . . . . . . . . . . 22 (26)"
*Finished length:* . . . . . . . . . . 15 (16)"
*Finished sleeve length:* . . . . . . 7½ (8½)"

## MATERIALS

- Tahki Cotton Classic (100% cotton, 50g/108yds)
  - ~ 6 (7) skeins #3446 (pink)
  - ~ 2 skeins #3525 (cream)
  - ~ 1 skein each #3711 (light green), #3997 (red)
- 1 pair size 3 US straight needles
- Stitch holder
- Stitch markers
- Tapestry needle
- 4 buttons

## GAUGE: 24 sts and 32 rows = 4" in St st

*Note: The following instructions are for the smaller size. The numbers for the larger size are given in parentheses. Where only 1 number is given, it applies to both sizes.*

## PATTERN STITCH
### Seed Stitch
Row 1: *K1, P1*; rep from * to * across.
All other rows: Knit the purl sts and purl the knit sts as they face you.

## BACK

With pink, CO 115 (134) sts. Work in St st until back is 9 (10)" long, ending with WS row facing for next row.

Dec row (WS): P3 (4), *P2tog, P2, P2tog, P3*; rep from * to * 12 (14) times, P2tog, P2 (3)—90 (105) sts.

## BACK YOKE

Next row (RS): With cream, work in P2, K1 ribbing across.

Next row (WS): Work in P1, K2 ribbing across.

Rep last 2 rows until back measures 14 (15)" long, ending with RS facing for next row.

## NECK SHAPING

Next row (RS): Work first 33 (36) sts in ribbing and put them on a st holder, BO off center 24 (33) sts, work last 33 (36) sts in ribbing.

Next row (WS): Working on last 33 (36) sts only, cont in ribbing as established.

Next row (RS): BO 9 sts at neck edge, work in ribbing to end.

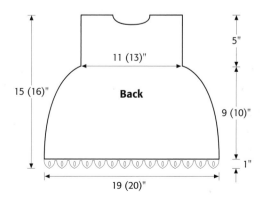

Next row (WS): Work in ribbing.

Next row (RS): BO 3 sts at neck edge, work in ribbing to end. BO all 21 (24) sts for shoulder. Cut yarn.

Next row (WS): Rejoin yarn at neck edge, BO 9 sts from st holder, work rem st from st holder in ribbing.

Next row (RS): Work in ribbing.

Next row (WS): BO 3 sts at neck edge, work in ribbing to end. BO all 21 (24) sts for shoulder.

## RIGHT FRONT

With pink, CO 57 (67) sts.

Row 1 (RS): Work first 6 sts in seed st, K to end.

Next row (WS): P to last 6 sts, work last 6 sts in seed st.

Rep last 2 rows until front measures 8 (9)" long, ending with RS facing for next row.

Buttonhole row (RS): Work in seed st as established for 2 sts, BO 2 sts for buttonhole, work in seed st for 2 sts, K to end.

Next row (WS): P to last 6 sts, work in seed st for 2 sts, CO 2 sts to complete buttonhole, work in seed sts for 2 sts.

Cont in seed st and St st as established until front measures 9 (10)" long, ending with WS facing for next row.

Dec row (WS): *P2tog, P2*; rep from * to * 12 (14) times, P3 (5), work in seed st for 6 sts, 45 (53) sts.

## RIGHT FRONT YOKE

Next row (RS): With pink, work first 6 sts in seed st, attach cream, and work in P2, K1 ribbing across.

*Note: As you cont making the right front, make 3 more buttonholes, spacing them 1 (1¼)" apart on the band of seed stitching.*

Cont in seed st and ribbing as established with 2 colors until piece measures 12½ (13½)" long, ending with RS facing for next row.

## NECK SHAPING

Next row (RS): BO 12 (14) sts, work in ribbing as established.

Next row (WS): Work in ribbing.

Next row (RS): BO 4 (5) sts, work in ribbing to end.

Next row (WS): Work in ribbing.

Next row (RS): BO 2 sts, work in ribbing to end.

Next row (WS): Work in ribbing.

Rep the last 2 rows 2 (3) more times.

Next row (RS): BO 1 st at neck edge, work in ribbing to end.

Next row (WS): Work in ribbing.

Next row (RS): BO 1 st at neck edge, work in ribbing to end—21 (24) sts.

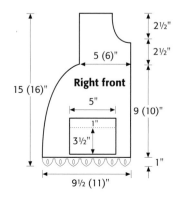

Cont in ribbing as established until front matches length of back, ending with RS facing for next row.

Next row (RS): BO all 21 (24) sts for shoulder.

## LEFT FRONT

With pink, CO 57 (67) sts.

Row 1 (RS): K to last 6 sts, work 6 sts in seed st.

Next row (WS): Work first 6 sts in seed st, P to end.

Rep last 2 rows until front measures 9 (10)" long, ending with WS facing for next row.

Dec row (WS): Work first 6 sts in seed st, P3 (5), *P2, P2tog*; rep from * to * 12 (14) times—45 (53) sts.

## LEFT FRONT YOKE

Next row (RS): With cream, work in P2, K1 ribbing to last 6 sts, attach pink, and work last 6 sts in seed st.

Cont in seed st and ribbing as established in 2 colors until piece measures 12½ (13½)" long, ending with WS facing for next row.

## NECK SHAPING

Next row (WS): BO 12 (14) sts, work in ribbing as established.

Next row (RS): Work in ribbing.

Next row (WS): BO 4 (5) sts, work in ribbing to end.

Next row (RS): Work in ribbing.

Next row (WS): BO 2 sts, work in ribbing to end.

Next row (RS): Work in ribbing.

Rep last 2 rows 2 (3) more times.

Next row (WS): BO 1 st at neck edge, work in ribbing to end.

Next row (RS): Work in ribbing.

Next row (WS): BO 1 st at neck edge, work in ribbing to end—21 (24) sts.

Cont in ribbing as established until front matches length of back, ending with WS facing for next row.

Next row (WS): BO all 21 (24) sts for shoulder.

## SLEEVES

Sew shoulder seams tog, referring to "Shoulder Seams" on page 25. Lay sweater on a flat surface, RS up. Place st markers at beg of yoke pat on front and back of sweater. With pink, pick up 72 (78) sts for sleeve between markers, taking care to space them evenly. Work in St st for 6½ (7½)", ending with RS facing for next row.

Next row (RS): *K2tog, K1*; rep from * to *—48 (52) sts.

Work in K1, P1 ribbing for 1". BO all sts.

Rep to make second sleeve at other armhole edge.

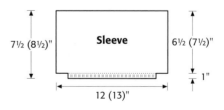

## POCKETS

With pink, CO 30 sts. Work in St st until pocket measures 3½" long, ending with RS facing for next row.

Next row (RS): Work in seed st for 1". BO all sts.

Rep to make second pocket.

## KNITTED LACE TRIM

With light green, CO 4 sts; K across these sts.

Row 1 (RS): K2, yo, K2.

Row 2 (WS): Sl 1, K across.

Row 3 (RS): K3, yo, K2.

Row 4 (WS): Rep row 2.

Row 5 (RS): K2, yo, K2tog, yo, K2.

Row 6 (WS): Rep row 2.

Row 7 (RS): K3, yo, K2tog, yo, K2.

Row 8 (WS): BO 4 st, K to end.

These 8 rows form the lace pat. Rep as many times as desired, ending with row 8; BO all sts. Make 2 lace trims, one long enough to fit along bottom edge of sweater and the other one long enough to fit around neck opening.

## FINISHING

To make smocking on yoke, thread a tapestry needle with a strand of pink yarn; from RS, count up 4 rows from beg of yoke and gather 2 K sts tog; repeat across width of yoke. Count up 4 more rows and make knots in the same manner, alternating them to create a diagonal smocked effect. Rep on both fronts and back.

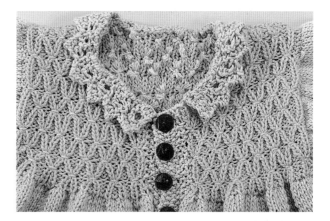

Sew pockets on sweater fronts, referring to "Pocket Seams" on page 26.

Sew underarm and side seams tog, referring to "Backstitch Seams" on page 25.

## ADDING THE BUTTONS

Sew 4 buttons on right front band, positioning them to match buttonholes on left front band. Overcast edges of buttonholes for durability, referring to "Making Buttonholes" on page 21.

## FRENCH KNOTS

With red, cream, and light green, add French knots to pockets as shown in photo on page 83. (See "French Knots" on page 29.)

## LACE TRIM

Sew lace trim around neckline and at bottom of sweater, referring to "Pocket Seams" on page 26.

# BERETS, BEANIE, AND HATS

FOUR-POINT BERETS

BOBBLE BEANIE

CHRISTMAS TREE HATS

# FOUR-POINT BERETS

I use the following
pattern to make
berets for toddlers and
children of any age.
(You can also use it
to make a matching
beret for yourself!)
Choose the same
colors I did, select
your favorite colors,
or use solid colors.
There are no rules;
whatever strikes your
fancy is fine!

**Size:** . . . . . . . . . . . . .Newborn to 6 mos.

## MATERIALS

- Tahki Cotton Classic (100% cotton, 50g/108yds)
  - ~ 1 skein of desired main color
  - ~ Scraps of contrast colors for decorative elements
- 16" size 3 US circular needle
- 4 size 3 US double-pointed needles
- Stitch markers
- Tapestry needle

## GAUGE: 24 sts and 32 rows = 4" in St st

## BOTTOM BAND

Determine the number of stitches you will need to cast on by measuring around the head of the child for whom you are knitting. Multiply this number (inches) times 6 (the correct knitting gauge per inch). Adjust your number up or down a few stitches as needed to make sure that it is divisible by 4 (the crown of the beret has four sides). Cast on the number of sts you need on the circ needle. Place a st marker on the right needle and join your cast-on sts tog, making sure that the sts do not become twisted on the needle.

Rnd 1: Purl.

Rnd 2: Drop first color yarn (but do not cut). Attach a second color yarn and *K1, sl 1 wyib, K1*; rep from * to * until you reach st marker.

Rnd 3: With the same color as in last rnd, *P1, sl 1 wyib, P1*; rep from * to * to marker.

Rnd 4: Drop the second color, pick up first color, and K around.

Rnd 5: Purl.

**TIP:** You can vary the number of rows you work for the bottom band, add more colors, or even knit more than one bottom band, separating the bands by rnds of St st, which can be embellished creatively later; see page 91 for ideas.

## SIDE BAND AND POINTS

With another color of your choice, K 11 rnds.

Next rnd: K, and divide your work into 4 equal sections, placing a st marker between each section.

Inc rnd: *K to 1 st before first st marker; K1f&b into that stitch; slip st marker onto right needle, K1, then K1f&b into *second* st from marker*; rep from * to * around.

Do 10 more inc rounds.

**TIP:** You can vary the number of knit rounds before you begin increasing to make the side band higher.

## TOP BAND

Rnd 1: With the same color as bottom band, knit.

Rnd 2: Purl.

Rnd 3: Drop first color yarn (but do not cut). Attach a new color yarn and *K1, sl 1 wyib, K1; rep from * to * around.

Rnd 4: With the same color as previous rnd, *P1, sl 1 wyib, P1*; rep from * to * around.

Rnd 5: Drop the second color and cut it. Pick up the first color; knit.

Rnd 6: Purl.

**TIP:** You can increase or decrease the number of rounds in your top band. You can also change colors, or you can eliminate the top band entirely and work 1 or more rounds in St st with a different color yarn.

## CROWN

Dec rnd: *K up to 2 sts before marker; K2tog, sl marker onto right needle, K1, K2tog*; rep from * to * around.

Cont working dec rnds in this manner, changing to 4 dpn when too few sts remain to cont using circ needle.

Next rnd: At this point, you can either BO all sts or finish with optional knitted cord (see page 91). For BO, when 8 sts remain, K2tog around, cut the yarn, and thread tail end through a tapestry needle to sew the sts tog, or finish the crown with a knitted cord.

## Finishing with a Knitted Cord

When 8 sts remain on dpn, keep working them using only 2 dpn, as follows: *K the sts, do not turn work. Instead, slide sts to right end of dpn, and pull yarn gently to tighten*. Rep from * to * until knitted cord is as long as you desire. BO all sts, cut the yarn, thread the tail end through a tapestry needle, and push needle down through center of knitted cord for a neat finish.

> **TIP:** You can make the knitted cord 1" to 2" long and add a button or bead at the end, or make the cord long enough that you can tie a knot at the top of the beret.

> **TIP:** To produce interesting concentric squares, use contrasting colors to work a pattern of stripes in the crown of the beret.

## CREATIVE EMBELLISHMENTS

Decorating children's berets is a lot of fun. Try some of these ideas, and enjoy coming up with some more of your own!

*Note: Consider the age of the child carefully when deciding whether or not to embellish a beret with buttons and beads, which present a choking hazard to small children.*

### Bobbles

With RS facing and main color, work to where you want the first bobble, drop main color yarn. With new color yarn, K1, P1, K1 in next st (making 3 sts from 1). Turn and K3. Turn and K3, lift second and third sts over first st. Drop the bobble yarn and pick up main color again. Work to next place for bobble, carrying the bobble yarn along the WS of work if the next bobble is 5 sts or less from the first bobble. Be sure to carry yarns loosely on WS to avoid distorting the knitting. If the bobbles will be more than 5 sts apart, cut the yarn after each bobble leaving a tail long enough to weave in, and start with a new strand of yarn for the next bobble.

### Spirals

CO 15 sts (or number to reach desired length of spiral).

Row 1: (K1f&b, K1) in each st.

Row 2: BO all sts pw. Rep to make as many spirals as desired; attach to top of crown.

## Pompons

You can decorate berets with a single pompon at each point or with a cascade of them, as you like. Use 1 color, 2 for a harlequin look, or lots of colors for a confetti effect. Refer to "Making Pompons" on page 30 for instructions.

## French Knots

Berets can be embellished with French knots in any color that strikes your fancy (see page 29). Use them on the side bands and crown, placing them wherever you like.

## Duplicate-Stitch Motifs

The following designs are great for decorating the side bands of a beret. Add them after you finish making the beret, referring to "Duplicate Stitching" on page 28. The number of sts in each rep is given on each chart; space the designs as needed to fit the number of sts in the side band of your beret. You can place the designs side by side or vary the number of sts between each motif.

**Star pattern**

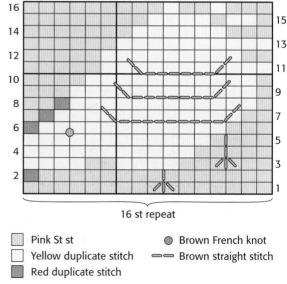

17 st repeat

- ■ Background St st
- □ Yellow duplicate stitch
- ● Green French knot

**Zigzag pattern**

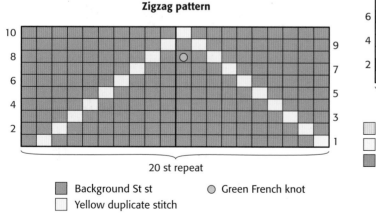

20 st repeat

- ■ Background St st
- □ Yellow duplicate stitch
- ● Green French knot

**Chick pattern**

16 st repeat

- Pink St st
- Yellow duplicate stitch
- Red duplicate stitch
- Brown French knot
- Brown straight stitch

**Beret pattern**

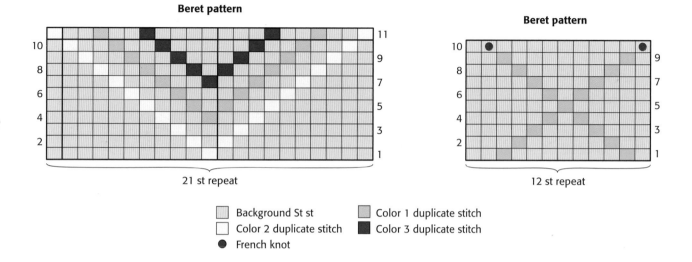

21 st repeat

**Beret pattern**

12 st repeat

◻ Background St st      ◻ Color 1 duplicate stitch
◻ Color 2 duplicate stitch      ◼ Color 3 duplicate stitch
● French knot

**Diagonal stripe pattern**

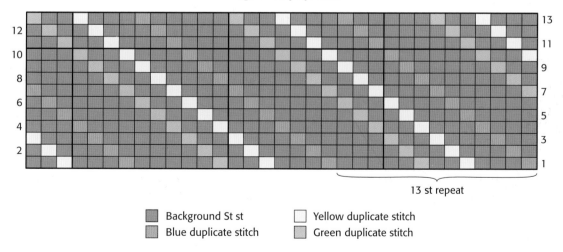

13 st repeat

◼ Background St st      ◻ Yellow duplicate stitch
◼ Blue duplicate stitch      ◻ Green duplicate stitch

# BOBBLE BEANIE

These playful little hats are a great place to use small amounts of leftover yarns in creative color combinations. Making them is a lot like eating potato chips—it's hard to stop at one!

*Size:* . . . . . . . . . . . Newborn to 6 mos.

## MATERIALS

- Tahki Cotton Classic (100% cotton, 50g/108yds)
  - ~ Small amounts of #3997 (red), #3553 (yellow), #3450 (pink), #3062 (blue), #3002 (black), and #3764 (green)
- 16" size 3 US circular needle
- 4 size 3 US double-pointed needles
- Stitch markers
- Tapestry needle

## GAUGE: 24 sts and 32 rows = 4" in St st

## PATTERN STITCH
### Bobbles

With RS facing in main color, work to place for first bobble, drop main color yarn. With new color yarn, K1, P1, K1 in next st (making 3 sts from 1). Turn and K3. Turn and K3, lift second and third sts over first st. Drop the bobble yarn and pick up main color again. Work to next place for bobble, carrying the bobble yarn along the WS of work. Be sure to carry yarns loosely on WS to avoid distorting the knitting.

**TIP:** To make a Bobble Beanie in a different size, use a tape measure to measure around the head of the child you are knitting for. Multiply this number (inches) times 6 (the correct knitting gauge per inch). Cast on this number of stitches (rounding up to an even number if your measurement yields an odd number) and follow the directions as given on these pages.

## RED-AND-YELLOW BOTTOM BAND

With circ needle and yellow, CO 102 sts. Place a st marker on right needle and join CO sts tog, making sure that sts do not become twisted on needle.

Rnd 1: Purl.

Rnd 2: Drop yellow yarn (but do not cut). Attach red yarn and *K1, sl 1 wyib*; rep from * to * around.

Rnd 3: *P1, sl 1 wyib*; rep from * to * around.

Rnd 4: With yellow, knit.

Rnd 5: Purl.

## RED-AND-YELLOW BOBBLE BAND

Rnds 1 and 2: With red, knit.

Rnd 3: *With yellow, make bobble in next st; with red, K5*; rep from * to * around.

Rnds 4 and 5: With red, knit.

## RED-AND-YELLOW BAND

Rep 5 rnds of red-and-yellow bottom band.

## GREEN-AND-BLUE BAND

Rnd 1: With green, purl.

Rnd 2: Drop green yarn (but do not cut). Attach blue yarn and *K1, sl 1 wyib*; rep from * to * around.

Rnd 3: *P1, sl 1 wyib*; rep from * to * around.

Rnd 4: With green, knit.

Rnd 5: Purl.

## GREEN-AND-BLUE BOBBLE BAND

Rnds 1 and 2: With blue, knit.

Rnd 3: *With green, make bobble in next st; with blue, K5*; rep from * to * around.

Rnds 4 and 5: With blue, knit.

## GREEN-AND-BLUE BAND

Rep 5 rnds of green-and-blue band.

## PINK-AND-YELLOW BAND

Rnd 1: With pink, purl.

Rnd 2: Drop pink yarn (but do not cut). Attach yellow yarn and *K1, sl 1 wyib*; rep from * to * around.

Rnd 3: *P1, sl 1 wyib*; rep from * to * around.

Rnd 4: With pink, purl.

Rnd 5: Knit.

## PINK-AND-YELLOW BOBBLE BAND

Rnds 1 and 2: With yellow, knit.

Rnd 3: *With pink, make bobble in next st, with yellow, K5*; rep from * to * around.

Rnds 4 and 5: With yellow, knit.

## PINK-AND-YELLOW BAND

Rep 5 rnds of pink-and-yellow band.

## BLACK TOP BAND

Rnd 1: With black, knit.

Rnd 2: *K6, K2tog*; rep from * to * around.

Rnd 3: *K5, K2tog*; rep from * to * around.

Rnd 4: *K4, K2tog*; rep from * to * around.

Rnd 5: *K3, K2tog*; rep from * to * around.

Rnd 6: *K2, K2tog*; rep from * to * around. Cont in this pat, changing to dpn when necessary. When 4 sts rem, BO all sts.

## ADDING THE SPIRALS

Referring to "Spirals" on page 91, make 5 spirals, each approximately 4" long, with green, pink, blue, red, and yellow. Sew them to the top of the beanie.

# CHRISTMAS TREE HATS

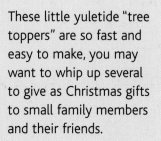

These little yuletide "tree toppers" are so fast and easy to make, you may want to whip up several to give as Christmas gifts to small family members and their friends.

| Size: . . . . . . . . . . . . Newborn to 6 mos. |
| --- |

## MATERIALS

- Tahki Cotton Classic (100% cotton, 50g/108yds)
  - ~ 1 skein #3726 (bright green) or #3744 (forest green)
  - ~ Small amounts of: #3997 (red), #3553 (yellow), and #3062 (teal)
- 16" size 3 US circular needle
- 4 size 3 US double-pointed needles
- Stitch markers
- Tapestry needle

## GAUGE: 24 sts and 32 rows = 4" in St st

## HAT BASE

With circ needle and green, CO 100 sts. Place a st marker on right needle and join CO sts tog, making sure that sts do not become twisted on needle.

Rnd 1: K, placing a st marker at halfway point of rnd.

Rnds 2–8: Knit.

Dec rnd: K to 2 sts from first marker, K2tog, K to 2 sts from second marker, K2tog.

Cont knitting each rnd, working a dec rnd on every other rnd. When 50 sts remain, beg working every rnd as a dec rnd, switching to dpn when necessary.

When 26 sts rem, K2tog around entire rnd. Rep until approx 6 sts remain. BO all sts. Cut the yarn, thread the tail end through a tapestry needle, and weave the yarn through several sts on WS of work.

## GARLANDS

With yellow, and referring to "Knitted Cords" on page 28, make a knitted cord that is long enough to wind around the hat several times, beg at the bottom edge and spiraling up to tip of hat. On WS, tack knitted garland in place with matching yarn.

> **TIP:** Just for fun, as you knit the rounds of the hat, you can knit 1 round in a contrasting color every so many rounds to form a knitted-in garland.

## POMPONS AND SPIRALS

Embellish tip of tree hat with colorful pompons, referring to "Making Pompons" on page 30, or add some knitted spirals, referring to "Spirals" on page 91.

## FRENCH KNOTS

With red, and referring to "French Knots" on page 29, add French knots to the hat, spacing them randomly between the garlands.

> **TIP:** To make a Christmas Tree Hat in a different size, use a tape measure to measure around the head of the child you are knitting for. Multiply this number (inches) times 6 (the correct knitting gauge per inch). Cast on this number of sts (rounding up to an even number if your measurement yields an odd number) and follow the directions as given on these pages.

# BOOTIES

BASIC BOOTIES

SWEET BOOTIES

FLOWER BOOTIES

MARY JANES

ANIMAL BOOTIES

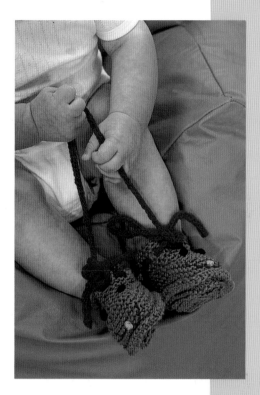

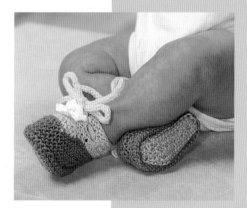

# BASIC BOOTIES

These booties are quite small, and made for babies to wear before they start to walk. Because baby booties tend to get themselves lost very easily, I like to make three booties in each style. They are quick and easy to make and lots of fun to decorate. Use the following basic bootie instructions for all of the booties shown in the photos and see if you can think up some more creative ways to embellish them.

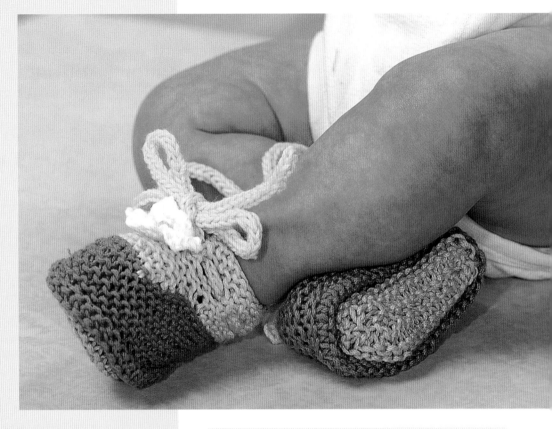

*Size:* . . . . . . . . . . . Newborn (3–6 mos.)

## MATERIALS

- Tahki Cotton Classic (100% cotton, 50g/108yds)
  - ~ Small amounts of leftover colors from other projects
- 1 pair size 3 US straight needles
- Stitch markers
- Stitch holders
- Tapestry needle

**GAUGE:** 24 sts and 32 rows = 4" in St st

*Note: The following instructions are for the smaller size. The numbers for the larger size are given in parentheses. Where only 1 number is given, it applies to both sizes.*

## PATTERN STITCH
### Garter Stitch
Knit all rows.

## TOP
CO 26 (34) sts for top portion of bootie.

Work 5 rows in garter st. Insert a st marker on the last row, to mark it as WS of bootie.

Beading row (RS): *K2, yo, K2tog*; rep from * to *, ending K2.

Work 5 (11) more rows (or as many rows as necessary to make the top part as long as desired) in garter st and cut yarn.

## INSTEP
Place the first 9 (12) sts on a st holder. Rejoin same color yarn as for bootie top, K across next 8 (10) sts for instep, place the last 9 (12) sts on a st holder, turn work.

Working on 8 (10) instep sts only, work 9 (11) rows in garter st, ending on WS row. Cut yarn.

Place first 9 (12) sts from st holder onto needle.

Row 1 (RS): Join new yarn, K9 (12) sts, pick up 9 (12) sts along side edge of instep, knit across 8 (10) instep sts, pick up 9 (12) sts along other side edge of instep, K9 (12) sts from second st holder—44 (58) sts.

Work 16 rows in garter st, ending with WS facing for next row.

## WELT
With WS facing, *sl the first st from the left to the right needle; count down 3 ridges on the WS of garter st rows, pick up and knit the top loop of the first st on this ridge, pass the first st over the new st*; rep from * to *—44 (58 sts).

Knit 1 row.

## SOLE
Row 1: With the same color, or a new color of your choice, K1, K2tog, K19 (26) sts, place st marker on needle; K to last 3 sts, K2tog, K1.

Row 2: Knit to 2 sts from st marker, K2tog, K1, K2tog, K to end.

Rep last row 4 times. BO all sts.

Rep from "Top" to make second (and third) bootie.

## FINISHING
Sew the seams of booties, referring to "Backstitch Seams" on page 25.

## KNITTED CORDS
Referring to "Knitted Cords" on page 28, CO 4 sts and make 1 knitted cord approximately 24" long for each bootie. Thread cord through beading row on each bootie and tie cord in a bow.

# Sweet Booties

This pair of booties coordinates with the Sweet Smock on page 80 and the pink Four-Point Beret with pompons on page 89.

## MATERIALS

- Tahki Cotton Classic (100% cotton, 50g/108yds)
  - ~ Small amounts of: #3446 (pink), #3711 (green), #3997 (red), and #3525 (cream)
- 1 pair size 3 US straight needles
- Stitch markers
- Stitch holders
- Tapestry needle

## GAUGE

24 sts and 32 rows = 4" in St st

## BOOTIES

Follow basic bootie instructions on page 103 to make small or large booties. Substitute seed st for garter st on top part of each bootie and use pink for instep and welt and green for soles. With green, make 1 knitted cord for each bootie, referring to "Knitted Cords" on page 28.

# Flower Booties

It takes only small amounts of brightly colored yarn to create these adorable booties.

# MATERIALS

- Tahki Cotton Classic (100% cotton, 50g/108yds)
  ~ Small amounts of desired colors
- 1 pair size 3 US straight needles
- Stitch holders
- Tapestry needle
- Stitch markers
- Size G or H crochet hook

# GAUGE

24 sts and 32 rows = 4" in St st

# BOOTIES

Follow the basic bootie instructions on page 103 to make small or large booties in the colors of your choice.

# FLOWERS

(Refer to instructions below as needed.)

To crochet a small flower: Make a chain of 6 sts; join into a circle. *Ch 3, 3dc into the circle, ch 3 and sc into the circle; rep from * 4 more times, sc into the circle. Cut yarn, thread the tail end through a tapestry needle, and weave it through a few sts on wrong side of the flower. Make a flower for each bootie and attach with a French knot to top of bootie.

## Chain Stitch

1. Make a slip knot in the yarn. Wrap the yarn over the hook and draw the yarn through the loop to form a new loop.

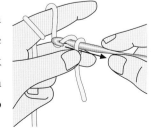

2. Repeat to form as many chains as required.

## Double Crochet

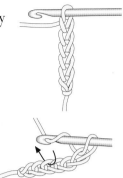

1. Wrap yarn around hook and insert the hook into the stitch.

2. Wrap yarn around hook and pull yarn through the stitch to the front of the work

3. Wrap yarn around hook and pull yarn through 2 loops on the hook.

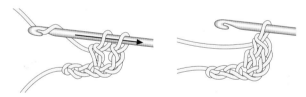

4. Wrap yarn around hook and pull yarn through 2 remaining loops on the hook.

# MARY JANES

The classic Mary Jane shoe takes on a playful air when made in miniature.

## MATERIALS

- Tahki Cotton Classic (100% cotton, 50g/108yds)
  ~ Small amounts of desired colors
- 1 pair size 3 US straight needles
- 1 button per bootie
- Stitch holders
- Tapestry needle
- Stitch markers

## GAUGE

24 sts and 32 rows = 4" in St st

## BOOTIES

Follow the basic bootie instructions on page 103 to make small or large booties.

To make strap: CO 3 sts. Work 10 rows in garter st. BO all sts. Rep to make a second strap. Sew straps to booties and add a button at one end of each strap.

# ANIMAL BOOTIES

Who could resist
these creative little
critters? Make them
in a rainbow of
colors to delight your
favorite little ones.

## MATERIALS

- Tahki Cotton Classic (100% cotton, 50g/108yds)
  ~ Small amounts of desired colors
- 1 pair size 3 US straight needles
- Stitch markers
- Stitch holders
- Tapestry needle

## GAUGE

24 sts and 32 rows = 4" in St st

## BOOTIES

Follow the basic bootie instructions on page 103 to make small or large booties. Add French knots (see page 29) to front of each bootie for a nose and eyes. Embroider a smile. If desired, make whiskers with scrap yarn. You can also make a very short spiral for a tail on each bootie.

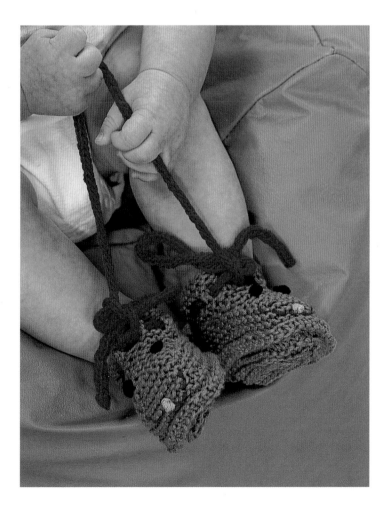

# ABOUT THE AUTHOR

Debby Ware discovered knitting as a child, when her mother taught her the basics, and she has loved it ever since. After graduating from the School of Visual Arts in New York City, she worked for various freelance designers knitting swatches, and she always loved to make one-of-a-kind sweaters for her family and friends. Eventually, she moved to Martha's Vineyard to work at her family's housewares gift store, Rainy Day, where she continued to knit and sell her unique sweaters for babies and young children. Becoming involved in a second family business on the Vineyard—renovating and running Alley's General Store—gave her another outlet for selling her creations. Later she started a small business of her own and has recently moved with her husband, Will, and son, Owen, to a large farm in Orange, Virginia, where she continues to follow her passions for both knitting and chickens.